Leonardo Weller

Sovereign Debt Crises and Negotiations in Brazil and Mexico, 1888-1914

Governments versus Bankers

palgrave
macmillan

Leonardo Weller
São Paulo School of Economics—FGV
São Paulo, Brazil

ISBN 978-3-030-08824-8 ISBN 978-3-319-73633-4 (eBook)
https://doi.org/10.1007/978-3-319-73633-4

Softcover re-print of the Hardcover 1st edition 2018

Cover design by Tom Howey

Printed on acid-free paper

This Palgrave Macmillan imprint is published by Springer Nature
The registered company is Springer International Publishing AG
The registered company address is: Gewerbestrasse 11, 6330 Cham, Switzerland

Sovereign Debt Crises and Negotiations in Brazil and Mexico, 1888-1914

To Nina and in memorian Waldemar

Preface

The relation between rich and poor countries is a hot topic among social scientists and the greater public. Centre–periphery, north–south and developed–developing are terms that characterise international economic relations in an unequal world. International finance is perhaps the most controversial channel of such uneven links. Governments in poor countries borrow the capital of rich economies on the sovereign debt market. For some, sovereign debt is a tool for economic development. For others, it is an instrument of international domination.

I grew up in Brazil in the 1980s. I was a schoolchild when my government defaulted on its sovereign debt. Together with very high inflation and stagnation, the debt crisis was one of the unfortunate features of Latin America's lost decade. My generation was taught that foreigners were the ones to blame for that economic nightmare. European and US bankers profited from attractive returns on our country's debt in the 1970s, and the IMF imposed unpopular policies in the 1980s. We have always been part of empires—so the argument goes—that existed to enrich the already rich elsewhere in the globe. The debt boom and crisis of that period were just a chapter of an old imperialistic story.

Governments and banks are major characters in that narrative, which depicts national leaders as malevolent and faint-hearted individuals who attended to the interests of global empires. International bankers were influential imperial masters. The names of presidents and finance ministers change, but the way they relate to the *haute finance* remains the same. That was probably why a history teacher told me at some point that the London House of Rothschild was the IMF of the past. As the reader will learn from this book, Rothschilds was Brazil's patron bank.

Similar messages are passed on across Latin America. Students in Mexico are bound to learn that international bankers colluded with Porfirio Díaz, the dictator who ruled the country at the turn of the twentieth century. One of Diego Rivera's most famous panels depicts Díaz besides two gentlemen dressed like European financiers, one of whom is literally eating gold coins. An insurgent from the Mexican Revolution rises above them. He looks determined to destroy that oppressive alliance.

I did a Ph.D. in Economic History at the London School of Economics. There I studied the liberal theories of the New Institutionalist Economics. It was not easy to conciliate the north–south tradition I had been embedded in with the new institutionalist literature. Who was to blame for Latin America's backwardness: international imperialism or regional institutions? Yet mainstream economic history coincides with some of the lessons of my anti-imperialistic background on the topic of sovereign debt. Eminent financial historians affirm that governments were creditworthy as long as they implemented the policies that the creditors preferred. New influential research concludes that premier banks had the power of choosing the market's favourite borrowers. The work of these scholars focuses on the supply side of the market; the governments—the demand side—were passive when negotiating loans. Officials accepted whatever creditors had to offer.

This monograph is based upon my Ph.D. The goal of my doctoral research was to assess the bargaining power of governments vis-à-vis bankers in the sovereign debt market of the first financial globalisation. I studied the relations of Brazil and Mexico with their debt underwriters from the 1880s to 1914. The period is relevant because it marks the establishment of the Brazilian Republic and the consolidation of the Mexican state under Díaz. Brazil was the best Latin American borrower until a republican coup deposed the monarchy in 1889. The government nearly defaulted a number of times in the 1890s and 1910s. Mexico, meanwhile, was the prototype of a failed state for most of the nineteenth century. Its debt remained unpaid until the Porfirian regime pacified the country and improved fiscal accounts. The Mexican government established a reputation as a borrower but defaulted after the Revolution toppled Díaz in the 1910s. If global bankers subjugated such remarkably different countries, the lessons of my youth and the bulk of the financial history literature are correct.

As I researched archives in Rio de Janeiro, Mexico City, London, Paris and Boston, I came to realise that these government–bank relations were much more balanced and nuanced than I had assumed. The governments of Brazil and Mexico were not passive when negotiating loans. They had the upper hand depending on the circumstances. The Mexicans chose not to have a patron bank, which allowed them to successfully bargain for better credit conditions with as many bankers as possible. Brazil's first republican administrations pressured Rothschilds into launching cheap loans that financed wars and prevented the debt from going into default. Given its reputational exposure to its client, the bank had no option but to throw good money after bad.

International bankers were not always masters of international finance: At crucial times, governments imposed their own terms. They did so by strengthening public finance and protecting the state. International market conditions alone did not determine the relations between governments and banker; the domestic political economy of borrowing countries also played a role. This book addresses the cases of Brazil and Mexico to show that the demand side of the sovereign debt market mattered.

São Paulo, Brazil — Leonardo Weller

Acknowledgements

I am grateful to Colin Lewis, who strongly supported my research and mentored me in the complex tasks of interpreting archive material and writing the dissertation that resulted in this book. Colin has thought me to allow primary evidence to speak for itself. I cannot exaggerate how important this has been (and will continue to be) to my career as an economic historian. I am indebted to Steven Haber and Rui Esteves, who have encouraged me to explore the full potential of the archive material I have collected. Bill Summerhill has so generously read my work in its very early and very late stages. I have benefited immensely from his valuable comments and persuasive arguments. Joe Francis has aided me throughout the process of writing this book, which would have been a poorer monograph without his detailed and insightful reading.

Many scholars have provided me with useful comments. In this list, I include Marcelo de Paiva Abreu, Sebastian Alvarez, Renato Colistete, Jordi Domènech, Leandro Prados de la Escosura, Juan Flores, Alejandra Irigoin, Leonor Ludlow, Renato Marcondes, Carlos Marichal, Aldo Musacchio, Luiz Carlos Prado, Paolo Riguzzi, Alexandre Saes, André Sant'Anna, Carlos Suprinyak, Antonio Tena and André Villela; my former colleagues and teachers at the London School of Economics Carlos Brando, Cecilia Lanata Briones, Chris Colvin, Francisco Costa, Chris Minns, Patrick O'Brien, Max Schulze, Peter Sims, Felipe Tâmega, Coskun Tunçer, Oliver Volckart and Bernardo Wjuniski; and my current colleges at the São Paulo School of Economics Luiz Felipe de Alencastro, Marcelo Fernandes, Emerson Marçal, Clemens Nunes, Daniel Monte, Verônica Orellano and Heleno Piazentini.

I have presented my research in a number of academic meetings where I had the chance of testing and developing its results. I thank the participants of the conferences, workshops and seminars organised by (in chronological order) the London School of Economics, All-University of California Economic History at Davis, Asociación Mexicana de Historia Económica, Associação Brasileira de Pesquisadores em História Econômica, Universidade de São Paulo, São Paulo School of Economics, Economic History Society, ESF-Globaleuronet Summer School, Economic History Association, the European Association for the History of Economic Thought, Congreso Latinoamericano de Historia Económica, Universitat Pompeu Fabra, Universitat Politècnica de Catalunya, Oxford University, Insper, Universidade Federal de Minas Gerais, Universitat Autònoma de Barcelona, Universidad Carlos III and Université de Genève.

I am indebted to the editors and referees of the *Journal of Economic History*, *Enterprise and Society* and *Economic History Review*, who have helped me to perfect articles that include fragments of this book. I quote my articles in the corresponding chapters.

I was fortunate to work in archives in Brazil, France, Mexico, UK and the USA. Leonor Ludlow, Alma Parra, and Paolo Riguzzi have guided me in Mexico City. My field research would have been difficult without their help. Finally, I thank the staff of the Rothschilds Archive, Archive Historique Paribas, Arquivo Nacional, Instituto Histórico e Geográfico do Brasil, Biblioteca Histórica do Ministério da Fazenda, Archivo Banamex, Archivo General Porfirio Díaz and Condumex for their kind support. I benefited from the London Stock Exchange Project, which was carried out by a research group from the Yale School of Management.

My research has been funded by CAPES, the Brazilian Agency for Higher Education. The London School of Economics and the Economic History Society have provided extra financial support.

Contents

List of Figures

List of Tables

PART I

Governments versus Bankers

CHAPTER 1

Introduction

The relations between governments and banks were at the very core of the sovereign debt market during the first financial globalisation, which lasted from the 1870s to the outbreak of the First World War. The banks in change of underwriting sovereign debt—obligations owned by central governments and denominated in foreign currency—arranged the issuing of bonds in international markets and the transfer of resources between borrowing governments and final creditors. The public associated governments with the banks in charge of underwriting their debt. As a consequence, defaults penalised both governments and banks: They restricted the formers' credit and downgraded the latters' status in the highly hierarchical debt underwriting business. Governments either negotiated loans with different banks or granted a monopoly on their debt—a decision that implied different payoffs. Negotiation reduced borrowing costs, while patron banking could improve the government's status, generate business opportunities and create a credit umbrella during crises.

By addressing the contrasting and complementary cases of Brazil and Mexico, this book demonstrates that governments adopted different approaches when dealing with the underwriters of their debt. Brazilian high officials handed a monopoly to the London Rothschilds, whereas the Mexicans did not accept patron-banking and negotiated cheap loans with many underwriters. This book assesses why these governments decided to relate to banks in such opposing ways.

This introductory chapter provides an overview of the interaction between governments and banks before 1914. The first section explains

L. Weller, *Sovereign Debt Crises and Negotiations in Brazil and Mexico, 1888-1914*, https://doi.org/10.1007/978-3-319-73633-4_1

the role of underwriters, and the second describes two major changes that transformed the market around the turn of the twentieth century. On the one hand, banks from continental Europe and the USA contested the dominant position that British underwriters had acquired since the market began in the 1820s. On the other hand, an information revolution enabled final bondholders to operate in a more independent way than in the 1820s, when they relied on banks to decide which bonds to buy. Together, these transformations increased the power of governments to foster competition among banks when negotiating borrowing terms. The remainder of this chapter outlines the book and previews the Brazilian and Mexican cases.

Governments and Banks in the First Financial Globalisation

The banks in charge of underwriting sovereign debt played a more important role in the past than today. In recent times, borrowing governments sell their bonds almost directly to a multitude of lenders who operate mostly online. Banks still underwrite bonds, participating in the issuing of new debt and the repayment of old obligations. However, as a general rule, the underwriting business does not involve much more than the transfer of resources from one side to another, charging relatively small fees for that service.

Banks played a crucial role in the pre-1914 sovereign debt market. The act of underwriting loans included some rather detailed tasks. Banks physically printed the bonds and organised their sale. They published announcements and news in the specialised press to attract final creditors, who bought and held the bonds. Banks collected periodical coupons, which the bondholders detached from the bonds and exchanged for interest payments. They also intermediated the payment of the debt's principal, helping the governments to buy back bonds as they reached maturity.

Technology partially explains why the process of debt underwriting was much more laborious in the past. The bonds were large pieces of paper and the handling of payments needed to be carried out *in loco*. Governments hired banks with branches in the cities that hosted international debt markets. It was common for a single loan to involve a group of underwriters—a syndicate—based in different places such as London, Paris, Brussels, Berlin and New York.

In the past, most contracts allowed the underwriters to buy the bonds from the government on the primary market and subsequently sell them at a different price on the secondary market. Contemporaries referred to such operations as taken under firm commitment. In some cases, the underwriters held the bonds for several months, expecting that improved market conditions would raise their price. With some luck (or inside information), bankers could realise some handsome profit from price run-ups.

Yet the business of debt underwriting differed from today in a more profound way than the simple act of issuing bonds and managing payments. The most important difference is that, in the past, the public identified the banks with the debt they underwrote and, more broadly, the governments that issued it. Today a Greek bond underwritten by Goldman Sachs is overall Greece's business. If the government in Athens defaults, it will face problems to borrow again—which, in some sense, has happened. Goldman Sachs would likely choose not to hold Greek debt, but the default would not disrupt the bank's activities.

That was less the case in the past. The banks of the first financial globalisation did not guarantee the debt they underwrote, but they did endorse it. The names of underwriters were printed on bonds. *The Investor's Monthly Manual*, the official publication of the London Stock Exchange, listed the debt issues traded on that market and reported their respective underwriters. In an article entitled "Bonds and Brands," Flandreau and Flores (2009) assert that, whenever they decided to underwrite the debt of a given country, high-class banks such as the London House of Rothschild (hereafter Rothschilds) sent signals to the public that operated on the secondary market. The Rothschilds "brand" indicated that associated governments were creditworthy. Second-class banks underwrote the debt of less credible borrowers; the good ones had been taken by premier underwriters. This hierarchical system among banks created a hierarchy of governments that determined the preferences of bondholders. According to this view, the underwriters were "gate keepers" that separated the worthy from the risky sovereign debt.[1]

It is possible to draw a parallel between the role of underwriters before 1914 and of credit agencies today. The credit rating business

[1] See also Flandreau and Flores (2010, 2012).

started when John Moody attributed rates to American railways' debt in 1908. Moody expanded its business to sovereign debt in 1918; Standard and Poor's and Fitch followed suit. Coincidence or not, the credit rating market begun just after the Soviets repudiated the Russian debt. The 1917 moratorium ruined Rothschilds' default-free brand forever—the old Russian Empire was Rothschilds' largest client. There is one significant difference between both activities, however: Underwriters used to face substantial losses when their clients defaulted, while credit agencies are not badly hurt when they get it wrong—they have done so greatly and are still in business. In this sense, traditional debt underwriting involved less conflict of interest than the business performed by credit agencies.[2]

Governments benefited from the association with premier banks. Brazil's bonds were attractive not only because of the country's capacity to meet payments but also due to Rothschilds' brand. Other countries did not have access to high-class banks because of their poor debt record. A previous serial defaulter, the Mexican government relied on the services of new underwriters from emergent markets in continental Europe and the USA. Yet Mexico borrowed as cheaply as Brazil in the 1900s. Thanks to a recently-acquired sound state finance, the Mexican government established a reputation among final creditors that enabled its negotiators to bargain for good borrowing terms with several different debt underwriters. In contrast to Brazil, which granted exclusivity to Rothschilds from the 1850s to 1908, Mexico never issued two consecutive loans with the same group of banks.

The Pre-1914 Sovereign Debt Market

The sovereign debt market had its international debut in the 1820s. The governments of a multitude of new countries borrowed in London, in a boom that followed the end of the Napoleonic Wars and the Latin American wars of independence. Nearly all borrowers suspended payments in that same decade. Weak guidance led investors to buy the bonds of Poyais, a country that did not exist. The underwriter, a Scottish impostor who had travelled around South America, made money by

[2]Chapter 8 will describe an intriguing exception: Mexico's 1913 loan, which was underwritten by Paribas and defaulted shortly afterwards. Evidence shows that the bank profited based on information asymmetry and conflict of interest.

selling bonds to creditors that never received any payment whatsoever (Sinclair 2004). At the other extreme of the market, Rothschilds underwrote the debt of Brazil, the only Latin American country that did not join that wave of defaults. Many banks disappeared as their clients suspended payments. Only Rothschilds and Barings survived the 1820s with default-free brands.

Rothschilds and Barings developed two different ways of doing business. The founder of the London house Nathan Rothschild built strong links with other banks and governments across Europe. The network included his siblings, who engaged in banking in Paris, Vienna and Naples. The Rothschilds from the continent provided their British relative with valuable inside information that largely explains their rise as global players. The London Rothschilds specialised in arbitrage and government finance as European powers waged war in the 1810s.[3] Barings operated in a less personalist way. It underwrote bonds of countries that became major destinations for foreign investment, such as the USA, Canada and, later in the nineteenth century, Argentina.[4] Rothschilds, in contrast, relied on its connections with traditional European monarchies. It became *the* bank of empires such as Austro-Hungary, Russia and Brazil, the only European monarchy in the new world.

Seniority was one of the keystones of the sovereign debt market. The banks that appeared after the 1820s were second rank underwriters that underwrote the bonds of newcomers and bad borrowers such as Mexico. Rothschilds inspired new banks in continental Europe that formed an informal international network. Chapman (1984, 36–37) refers to these financiers as "court Jews." That was the case of Gerson Bleichroeder, a banker from Berlin who was in charge of managing Bismarck's fortune (Stern 1979, 426–27). This traditional banking expanded to the USA, where Edward Speyer funded a house that operated on international public finance (Carosso and Sylla 1991, 60–61). As will be detailed in this book, Bleichroeder and Speyers attempted (and failed) to become Mexico's patron banks. The market also included larger universal banks such as Paribas, which underwrote sovereign debt to diversify away from its businesses in France (Bonin 2002).

[3]See Jones (1987) and Ferguson (1998) for more on the early years of the London House and its relation with the continental Rothschilds.

[4]See Austin (2007) for more on Barings.

The sovereign debt market became larger, more global and competitive by the turn of the twentieth century. The resources of single banks were too limited for the growing demand for credit, which explains the rise of international syndicates. Even though syndicates had been issuing loans since the 1820s, by circa 1900 they became the rule. In the earlier period, banks like Barings and Rothschilds avoided competition by picking different countries, such as Argentina and Brazil, respectively. After the 1890s, members of the syndicate cooperated, but different syndicates competed for good deals. This book will show that Speyer and Paribas formed syndicates to compete over Mexican loans in the 1900s. Brazil broke Rothschilds' monopoly in that same decade, when it issued bonds in Paris through syndicates composed of Paribas and other French banks. The new underwriters not only approached previous defaulters such as Mexico, occupying a share of the market that premier banks would not enter; they also competed with Rothschilds in its niche.

Another major transformation was the technological progress in communication and data processing, particularly in the last quarter of the nineteenth century. International telegraphic cables improved the capacity of the final creditors that operated in secondary market to access data on the political and financial conditions of the borrowing countries. Newspapers such as *The Times* and *The Economist* published an increasing amount of financial and political news from around the globe. Periodicals such as *Statesmen's Yearbook* compiled annual data on virtually every country in the world. Bondholders were not so much in the dark as they had been in the 1820s. They could rely on their judgment instead of being entirely dependent on underwriters for gatekeeping. The turning point was the Baring Crisis of 1890, which begun with an Argentinean default that technically bankrupted Barings, that country's major underwriter. The crisis nearly caused a systemic financial meltdown in London. It became evident that the Barings brand was not as good as the public had believed (Mauro et al. 2006, 11–12).

The French bank Crédit Mobilier seized this opportunity to develop a credit risk research department in the 1890s. It aimed to tell clients which bonds to buy based on objective analysis (Flandreau and Zumer 2004, 27–28, 51–54). That did not mean, however, that the old way of doing business, based on long-lasting relations and reputation, disappeared altogether. Both traditional and modern sovereign debt intermediation coexisted in the booming sovereign debt market of the

Belle Époque. Final creditors started to assess risk objectively, yet the brands of premier banks still mattered, although less than before. It was only after the First World War that the Rothschilds brand started to become irrelevant.

The rise of competition among banks and the improvement in information quality benefited borrowing governments. For most of the nineteenth century, governments needed to access the brand of a good bank to borrow cheaply; by the turn of the century, they could build a reputation of their own by running sound finance. Borrowers depended less on prestigious banks because they could negotiate good deals with competing second-rank underwriters. Governments became more powerful than before and, depending on the conditions, had the upper hand over banks.

Book Outline

This book analyses how the governments of Brazil and Mexico negotiated loans with the banks in charge of underwriting their debt. These case studies provide pronounced contrasts: Brazil was an established borrower that almost defaulted a number of times, while Mexico was a debt delinquent that returned to the market and established a reputation. In spite of such differences, the analysis of these cases supports the following conclusion: Governments played an active role in negotiating the terms at which they borrowed abroad.

The changes in the sovereign debt market during the first financial globalisation empowered governments. It was up to the Brazilian and Mexican negotiators to devise specific strategies to take advantage of these transformations. The options and strategies were different, but the goal was the same: to protect the interests of the state when borrowing abroad.

The book's major findings complement the literature on sovereign debt, which by and large focuses on the ways banks and bondholders decided to lend rather than the action of governments when borrowing. This work is at odds with the widespread view that international bankers have always had the upper hand over borrowing governments. The financial history of Brazil and Mexico shows that the relations between governments and banks were much more balanced and nuanced than is generally assumed.

The book is composed of three parts. Part I presents the book's historical and analytical framework. It includes this introduction and Chapter 2. Parts II and III address the Brazilian and Mexican cases, respectively. They include three chapters each, which describe the relations between these countries' governments and banks in chronological order.

Part I—Governments versus Bankers

Part I introduces the main question of the book: How did governments and banks negotiate the issuing of sovereign loans in the first financial globalisation. This chapter described how the sovereign debt market functioned before 1914. Based on this historical overview, Chapter 2 analyses the literature on sovereign debt and identifies the book's main contributions. The bulk of the theoretical and historical literature focuses on the supply side of the market. With few exceptions, financial historians tend to portray governments as passive or weak vis-à-vis banks. They generally give the impression that governments only influenced the way the market worked by running sound policies and repaying their debt. It was up to the bankers to decide how much and at what conditions to lend. In contrast, this book addresses the relations of Brazil and Mexico with their debt underwriters from the point of view of the banks as well as the governments.

Chapter 2 introduces the analytical framework of the book. It identifies factors that defined the relative power of governments vis-à-vis banks. The balance between borrowers and lenders determined how effectively each side negotiated loans. Governments were stronger the better their reputation among the bondholders. A worthy reputation—resulting from a good debt record, the association with premier banks, political stability and sound finance—allowed them to bargain for better deals with the banks that underwrote debt on the primary market.

Banks were stronger the higher their status as debt underwriters. Governments were more likely to grant exclusivity to premier banks, as such an association would increase their own reputation. That would come at a cost, for governments would not be able to negotiate with other banks. Second-class underwriters would find it harder to establish a monopoly over a country's debt because they provided a weaker set of benefits to their exclusive clients.

Besides reputation, exposure also determined the banks' relative power. A bank that had underwritten too many loans of a single government would become weak when the latter faced debt crises. Troubled clients could threaten to default to force highly exposed banks to lend cheaply. I define such operations as rescue loans: Credit facilities issued at risk premium below the market rate during crises. Rescue loans entailed opportunity costs; the wore the crisis, the greater the costs. The higher the status of the exposed banks, though, the more there was at stake in the event of defaults. In such circumstances, governments had considerable leverage in negotiating the issuing of rescue loans. In other words, high-class banks tended to become weaker than mediocre ones when governments were on the edge of defaulting the debt they had underwritten.

Parts II—Brazil versus Rothschilds

Chapter 3 describes how the Brazilian Empire built a long-lasting association with Rothschilds since the 1820s. Among all new borrowers that appeared on the market in that decade, Rothschilds chose Brazil as its Latin American client. The government appointed Rothschilds as its financial agent and granted a monopoly on the underwriting of its debt in the 1850s. The agreement improved Brazil's status among final creditors, who associated Brazilian bonds to Rothschilds.

Table 1.1 lists the loans Brazil issued from the 1820s to 1914. Rothschilds' position as Brazil's patron bank stands out in the table, which also shows that the government borrowed extensively in the second half of the nineteenth century. The underwriting of Brazilian loans made Rothschilds exposed. By the time a republican coup toppled the monarchy, in 1889, 31% of all the foreign bonds Rothschilds had ever underwritten on its own were Brazilian (Ayers 1905). A default on the Brazilian debt would not immediately ruin Rothschild financially, as the bank held a small share of the bonds it underwrote. However, it would destroy its reputation—the very core of its business—with severe long-term financial consequences.

Chapter 4 addresses the Brazilian debt crisis of the 1890s. The new republican governments implemented loose monetary policies, wars deteriorated fiscal accounts and the price of coffee fell. Brazil would have defaulted had Rothschilds not underwritten rescue loans. The chapter analyses official correspondence to show that Rothschilds' exposure

Table 1.1 Brazilian sovereign loans, 1824–1914 (*Source BHMF* 332/225-6 for the lending contracts; *The Investor's Monthly Manual* for the British consol)

	Underwriter	*Amount (£ million)*	*Risk premium (%)*	*Use of resources*
1824–5, 5%	Crawford, Alexander, Wilson, Rothschilds	5.09	3.11	Fiscal deficit
1825, 5%	Rothschilds	1.40	2.77	Portuguese debt
1829, 5%	Rothschilds, Wilson	0.77	6.79	Debt service
1839, 5%	Phillips	0.41	3.66	Debt service
1843, 5%	Goldmid	0.73	3.20	Portuguese debt
1852, 4.5%	Rothschilds	1.04	1.58	Portuguese debt
1854, 5%	Rothschilds	3.17	1.78	Conversion
1858, 4.5%	Rothschilds	1.53	1.76	Railways
1859, 5%	Rothschilds	0.51	1.84	Portuguese debt
1860, 4.5%	Rothschilds	1.37	1.97	Railways
1863, 4.5%	Rothschilds	3.86	2.07	Debt conversion
1865, 5%	Rothschilds	6.96	3.77	Paraguayan War
1871, 5%	Rothschilds	3.46	2.55	Domestic debt
1875, 5%	Rothschilds	5.30	1.98	Railways
1883, 4.5%	Rothschilds	5.40	2.20	Fiscal deficit
1886, 5%	Rothschilds	6.43	2.34	Domestic debt
1888, 4.5%	Rothschilds	6.30	1.70	Emancipation
1889, 4%	Rothschilds	19.84	1.50	Debt conversion
1893, 5%	Rothschilds	3.70	3.75	War, railways
1895, 5%	Rothschilds	7.40	3.53	Debt service
1898, 5%	Rothschilds	8.60	1.50	Debt service
1901, 4%	Rothschilds	16.60	3.12	Railways
1903, 5%	Rothschilds	5.50	2.54	Public works
1906, 5%	Rothschilds	1.10	2.77	Brazilian Lloyd
1908, 5%	Rothschilds	4.00	2.69	Conversion, public works
1908, 5%	S. Géneral, Paribas	4.00	2.16	Railways
1909, 5%	C. Mobilier	1.60	2.29	Public works
1910, 4%	Rothschilds	10.00	1.58	Conversion, railways
1910, 4%	C. Mobilier, Paribas	4.00	1.53	Railways
1910, 4%	Rothschilds	1.00	2.06	Brazilian Lloyd
1911, 4%	Rothschilds	4.50	1.62	Public works
1911, 4%	Caisse C. I.	2.40	1.77	Railways
1911, 4%	Lloyds	2.40	1.69	Railways
1913, 5%	Rothschilds	11.00	1.85	Services, public works
1914, 5%	Rothschilds, D. Geselschaft, S. Génerale, Paribas	14.50	1.67	Debt service

allowed Brazil to free-ride on its credit umbrella. High officials relied on the bank to launch policies that attended political goals at the expenses of the fiscal accounts.

The pacification of Brazil in the late 1890s created the conditions the government needed to bring the debt crisis to an end. The government intended to re-establish payment capacity, which became a peacetime priority. Finance Minister Bernardino de Campos (1896–1898) suggested a rescuing package known as the Funding Loan, which was launched in 1898. Bernardino de Campos proposed to pay interests due on the debt with newly issued bonds rather than cash for three years. In return, the government would burn paper currency to strengthen the exchange rate. At first, Rothschilds refused the deal, but the bankers reconsidered once the minister threatened to suspend payment unilaterally. Rothschilds played the role of a power broker between a newly elected administration and the lobbyists of the coffee sector, whose profitability fell as the exchange rate appreciated.

Having lost with the policies introduced in the Funding Loan, the coffee lobby pressured the state of São Paulo to launch the first price stabilisation programme at a global level in 1906. São Paulo produced over half of the world's coffee supply. The government of that state borrowed in New York to finance a large-scale stockpiling initiative, but that year's harvest was so abundant that São Paulo alone failed to fund the scheme. Chapter 4 shows that the *Paulistas* pressured the federal government to borrow from Rothschilds to support the programme. The bankers publicly opposed the stockpiling of coffee, but they agreed to transfer funds to São Paulo. Rothschilds had to intervene because the coffee sector was too important for Brazil.

Coffee became a problem again in 1913 when another large harvest depressed prices. São Paulo lacked the financial capacity to launch a second valorisation programme. Brazil's currency *mil-réis* depreciated and customs revenue fell. The government proposed a new Funding Loan along the lines of the rescuing package of 1898. Similarly to what had happened before, Rothschilds at first repudiated the deal but complied after the Brazilians threatened to default. The blackmail became rather convincing in mid-1914, when the outbreak of the First World War reduced short-term credit, deteriorating Brazil's payment capacity even further. Differently from the 1890s, this new debt crisis was related to the volatility of the coffee market, which explains why Rothschilds did not condition the Second Funding Loan on the adoption of orthodox policies.

Rothschilds rescued the Brazilian government even though the latter had broken the former's monopoly in 1908, when it issued loans in Paris. Brazil took advantage of its good reputation and the rise in liquidity of the *Belle Époque* to cut deals that involved lower commission with French banks. It is noteworthy that the diversification of borrowing sourced did not compromise the government's ability to negotiate a rescue loan with Rothschilds in 1914.

Lending conditions synthesise the changes of Brazil's relations with Rothschilds as well as with the final bondholders. Figure 1.1 reports the risk premium at which Brazil borrowed from the 1880s to 1914. Risk premium is the cost of borrowing, defined as the difference between the return on a given bond and on the Britain's long-term public debt, the British consol, which was the benchmark of the time. The dots in the graph are the risk premium applied to every Brazilian loan, which are also shown in Table 1.1. They are plotted in the months of signature of these loans' contracts. The solid line is Brazilian risk, the risk premium applied to all Brazilian bonds floating on the London Stock Exchange. Data Appendix provides a formal definition of risk premium and country

Fig. 1.1 Brazilian risk and risk premium applied to sovereign loans (*Source BHMF* 332/225-6 for the lending contracts; *The Investor's Monthly Manual* for the bonds floating in London and the British consol)

risk. Brazilian risk increased steeply in the turbulent 1890s as politics became unstable and fiscal accounts deteriorated. The Funding Loan was issued at a 2.5% risk premium, way below Brazilian risk, which was at 7.5%. Similar lending happened in 1893 and 1914, although the difference between the primary and secondary market rates was not so wide.

The 1893, 1898 and 1914 loans were issued below Brazilian risk, while most other lending facilities were issued above it. According to the initial offer condition, new loans are expected to yield higher return than old debt to compensate for seniority—to attract creditors that believe that, in case of default, the government would first suspend payment on newer bonds (Miller and Reilly 1987). The reason why the 1898 and 1914 loans were cheap relative to the market rate is that they were rescue loans, designed to prevent the government from defaulting. I discuss this concept further in Chapter 2.

Part III—Mexico versus Mediocre Banks

Mexico was among the world's worst borrowers until Porfirio Díaz (1876–1880, 1884–1911) took office. Chapter 6 reviews Mexico's serial defaults from the 1820s until the 1880s, a period during which the country was isolated from international finance. The first part of the chapter explains the causes of debt mismanagement: The failure of Mexico as a nation-state. While Brazil had two emperors and seven regents during the six-decade-long monarchic era, Mexico had on average almost two heads of state per year from independence, in 1821, to the late 1860s, when politics started to stabilise. Nearly all world powers took advantage of the constant state of civil war between liberals and conservatives. The USA incorporated half of Mexico's territory, Spain and Britain took port cities and French troops invaded Mexico City. France imposed the rule of the Austrian noblemen Maximilian (1864–1867), whose short-lived administration issued loans in Paris. Republican forces deposed the invasion and repudiated that debt.

The second part of Chapter 6 analyses how the country returned to the financial market in the early years of Díaz's dictatorship, which established peace and virtually built a state from scratch. His government arranged a settlement with foreign creditors and subsequently issued a loan abroad in 1888. The chapter shows that Bleichroeder, the leading underwriter, profited handsomely from that operation and intended to become Mexico's patron bank. The banker understood that the country was pacifying and expected that the price of Mexican bonds would increase. Díaz accepted to issue the 1888 loan at relatively poor conditions but contracted another loan through different banks at better terms in the following year. Bleichroeder failed to convert Mexico into a stable source of rent.

Mexico would not have benefited from an exclusive association with Bleichroeder as much as Brazil did with Rothschilds. There was no comparison between these two banks' statuses. The nationalistic ideology of the Porfirian state also explains why the Mexicans refused to have a patron bank. After decades of foreign invasions, high officials were reluctant to depend too much on a single foreign company. For the next three decades, Mexico contracted the services of different syndicates every time it borrowed abroad. This stands out from Table 1.2, which details Mexico's sovereign loans from 1823 to 1913. The Mexican government had the highest underwriter turnover in the world under Díaz, while Brazil had the lowest (Flores 2012, 19).

Table 1.2 Mexican sovereign loans, 1823–1913 (*Source* Casasús (1880), Payno (1868) and Mexico (1925) for the lending contracts; *The Investor's Monthly Manual* for the British consol)

Loans	*Underwriters*	*Amount (£ million)*	*Risk premium (%)*	*Use of revenue*
1823, 6%	Goldschmidt	3.2	4.87	Deficit
1825, 5%	Berkley	3.2	3.48	Deficit
1864, 6%	Peréire, Glyn Mills	7.8	6.20	Debt service
1865, 6%	Peréire, Glyn Mills	7.8	6.17	Services
1988, 6%	Bleichroeder, Gibbs	10.5	4.85	Conversion
1889, 5%	Dresdner, Seligman	2.7	3.53	Railways
1890, 6%	Bleichroeder, Gibbs	6.0	4.01	Railways
1893, 6%	Bleichroeder, Glyn Mills	3.0	6.06	Debt service
1899, 5%	Bleichroeder, Dresdner, Morgan Grenfell, JP Morgan	22.7	2.68	Conversion
1904, 4%	Speyers	8.2	1.73	Railways
1910, 4%	1899 Syndicate, Paribas, C. Lyonnais, S. Générale, C. Nationale	22.2	1.27	Conversion
1912, 4.5%	Speyers	2.0	12.81	Debt service
1913, 6%	1910 syndicate	6.0	4.08	Debt service
1913, 4.5%	Speyers	2.0	12.74	Debt service

Mexico borrowed at rather expensive conditions as it re-entered the market in the late 1880s. This appears in Fig. 1.2, which also shows that Mexican risk reached a maximum during the silver crisis of the early 1890s. Silver prices collapsed, severely compromising the government's accounts. The peso was pegged to silver, which was also the country's main exporting commodity. Chapter 7 describes that Mexico emerged from the crisis with a new reputation. Cheap silver depreciated the exchange rate and boosted merchandise trade. Díaz privatised indigenous lands, which was disgraceful for native communities but created an elastic supply of labour for the booming agricultural, mining and industrial sectors. As the economy grew, the government introduced new taxes and ran a sustainable fiscal policy. The most prominent policymaker of the Porfiriato, Finance Minister Yves Limantour (1893–1911) defended sound accounts as a way to make the state strong enough to protect Mexico's sovereignty. While Díaz's generation took in arms against foreign invaders (the president was a general), Limantour raised taxes, cut expenditure and negotiated cheap loans. Fiscal accounts became sound and Mexican risk decreased in the second half of the 1890s, reaching low levels in the 1900s.

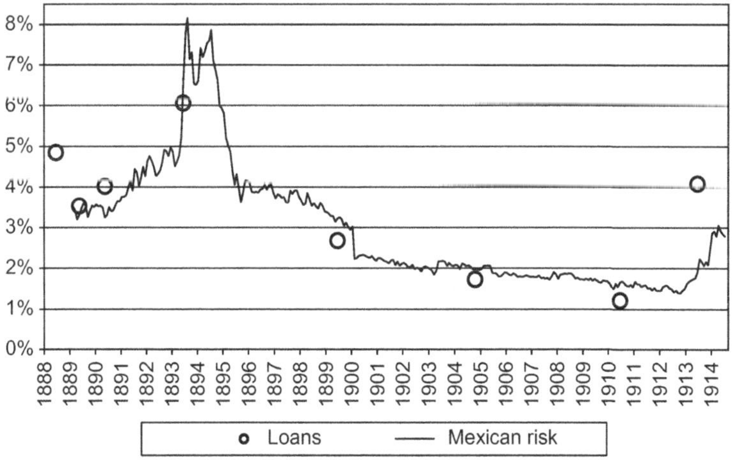

Fig. 1.2 Mexican risk and risk premium applied to sovereign loans (*Source* Mexico (1925) for the lending contracts; New York Stock Exchange for the 1904 bonds; Bulletin de la Côte for the 1910 bonds; *The Investor's Monthly Manual* for all other Mexican bond issues and the British consol)

Borrowing terms improved significantly between 1899 and 1910, when the government issued loans at risk premiums below Mexican risk. That was the result of active negotiation. Chapter 7 shows that Minister Limantour fomented the competition among bankers to improve credit conditions. The banks that underwrote these loans attempted to buy the bonds from the government at low price to sell them at a margin on the secondary market. Limantour bargained to lift the issuing prices, squeezing the underwriter's profitability and raising the government's revenue. He did so by negotiating the loans with as many bankers as possible. The minister used the aggressive offers of US banks as a bargaining tool when dealing with more established European underwriters.

The Revolution that deposed Porfirio Díaz in 1911 escalated into a civil war that caused a debt crisis. The government defaulted and the state subsequently collapsed in 1914. Chapter 8 explains how the respectively revolutionary and counter-revolutionary administrations of Madero (1911–1913) and Huerta (1913–1914) borrowed in spite of the political turmoil. Considerably expensive, the loans of the Revolution contributed to the deterioration of fiscal accounts and help to explain why Mexico suspended payments in 1914. The government was in a weak position to negotiate.

Paribas, the head of the syndicate that underwrote the 1913 loan, had access to inside information on the country's very volatile political conditions. Still influenced by the Porfiriato's peace and progress, the general public expected that the country would soon pacify. Paribas purchased the bonds at a high discount from the government and quickly sold them at a profit on the secondary market. Asymmetry of information explains why the loan was issued so much above Mexican risk, as shown in Fig. 1.2. Paribas had no financial exposure whatsoever when the government defaulted. This is a case of a troubled government that failed to receive the credit it needed not to default. The loans of the Mexican Revolution contrast with the rescue loan Rothschilds granted to Brazil in that same period. Limantour's strategy of bargaining for better borrowing terms worked during the Porfiriato but left Presidents Madero and Huerta without a patron bank that would provide a credit umbrella in the difficult times of the Revolution.

References

Archival Sources

BHMF Biblioteca Histórica do Ministério da Fazenda, Rio de Janeiro.
Contractos dos empréstimos em libras esterlinas do Governo Federal, 1883 a 1927, 332/225.
Contractos dos empréstimos em francos e em dollar do Governo Federal, 1883 a 1927, 332/226.

Official and Contemporary Sources

Ayers, Jules. 1905. *A Century of Finance, 1804 to 1904: The London House of Rothschild*. London: Neely.

Bulletin de la Côte

Casasús, Joaquín Demetrio. 1880. *Historia de la deuda contraída en Londres, con un apéndice sobre el estado actual de la hacienda pública*. Mexico City: Imprenta del Gobierno.

Mexico. 1925. *Coleccion de leyes y disposiciónes relaciónadas con la deuda exterior de Mexico*. Mexico City: Secretaría de Hacienda y Crédito Público.

New York Stock Exchange

Payno, Manuel. 1868. *Cuentas, Gastos, Aceedores y Otros Asuntos Del Tiempo de La Intervencion Francesa y Del Imperio*. Mexico City: Ignacion Cumplido.

The Investor's Monthly Manual

Secondary Sources

Austin, Peter E. 2007. *Baring Brothers and the Birth of Modern Finance*. London: Routledge.

Bonin, Hubert. 2002. "The Political Influence of Bankers and Financiers in France in the Years, 1850–1960." In *Finance and Financiers in European History 1880–1960*, edited by Youssef Cassis, 219–42. Cambridge: Cambridge University Press.

Carosso, P. Vincent, and Richard Sylla. 1991. "U.S. Banks in the International Finance." In *International Banking: 1870–1914*, edited by Rondo E. Cameron and Bovykin, V. Ivanovich, 48–71. Oxford: Oxford University Press.

Chapman, Stanley D. 1984. *The Rise of Merchant Banking*. New York: Routledge.

Ferguson, Niall. 1998. *The World's Banker: The History of the House of Rothschild*. New York: Weidenfeld & Nicolson.

Flandreau, Marc, and Frédéric Zumer. 2004. *The Making of Global Finance 1880–1913*. Paris: OECD.

Flandreau, Marc, and Juan H. Flores. 2009. "Bonds and Brands: Foundations of Sovereign Debt Markets, 1820–1830." *The Journal of Economic History* 69 (3):646–84.

———. 2010. Hamlet Without the Prince of Denmark: Relationship Banking and Conditionality Lending in the London Market for Foreign Government Debt, 1815–1913. IHEID Working Papers 8-2010.

———. 2012. "Bondholders Versus Bond-Sellers? Investment Banks and Conditionality Lending in the London Market for Foreign Government Debt, 1815–1913." *European Review of Economic History* 16 (4):356–83.

Flores, Juan H. 2012. "Fundamentos Económicos, Fallos de Mercado y Exportación de Capitales: América Latina y El Mercado de Londres, 1880–1913." *América Latina En La Historia Económica* 19 (3): 5–30.

Jones, Charles A. 1987. *International Business in the Nineteenth Century: The Rise and Fall of a Cosmopolitan Bourgeoisie*. New York: Wheatsheaf Books.

Mauro, Paolo, Nathan Sussman, and Yishay Yafeh. 2006. *Emerging Markets and Financial Globalization: Sovereign Bond Spreads in 1870–1913 and Today*. Oxford: Oxford University Press.

Miller, Robert E., and Frank K. Reilly. 1987. "An Examination of Mispricing, Returns, and Uncertainty for Initial Public Offerings." *Financial Management* 16 (2):33–38.

Sinclair, David. 2004. *The Land That Never Was: Sir Gregor Macgregor and the Most Audacious Fraud in History*. Cambridge, MA: Da Capo Press.

Stern, Fritz. 1979. *Gold and Iron: Bismark, Bleichroder, and the Building of the German Empire*. New York: Vintage.

CHAPTER 2

Governments versus Bankers in the Pre-1914 Sovereign Debt Market

The bulk of the literature on sovereign debt focuses on the supply side of the market—the banks that underwrite loans and the final creditors that hold bonds—rather than the role governments played in sovereign debt negotiations. The theory that emerged in the 1980s, following that decade's Latin American debt crisis, concludes that creditors will lend to governments that implement orthodox economic policy in politically stable countries. Governments are independent domestically, where they determine economic policies and condition national politics, but are submissive in the global market, where they borrow without negotiating credit conditions. An influential historical literature follows this approach when it asserts that countries that joined the Gold Standard to attract cheap credit. The same applies to the more recent scholarship that highlights the role of debt underwriters, which shifts the centre of decision-making from bondholders to banks. Flandreau and Zumer (2004, 58) acknowledge that they do not study the demand side of the market, which they define as "the governments' borrowing policies."

I make the case that governments were independent players in the first financial globalisation. This point appears in the work of a few authors, but they have not developed it further to assess the rationale of the governments' decision-making when they approached debt underwriters.[1] I address this gap in this chapter. Governments were free to decide whether to grant exclusivity to a single patron bank or to negotiate with

[1] This chapter will provide a detailed literature review.

L. Weller, *Sovereign Debt Crises and Negotiations in Brazil and Mexico, 1888-1914*, https://doi.org/10.1007/978-3-319-73633-4_2

competing banks to reduce borrowing costs. Both options entailed costs and benefits. Patron banks could raise the governments' reputation and create business connections in key sectors such as railways, generating spillovers from the issuing of sovereign debt. Exclusivity also increased the chances that banks would grant cheap credit in times of crisis to prevent their clients from defaulting—an operation I call rescue loan. By agreeing on exclusivity, however, governments would not bargain for lower commission and higher issuing price. Governments were likely to grant exclusivity to premier banks if the prospect of negotiating better deals was limited. The inverse happened when governments could not access high-class banks but were able to promote competition among second-class underwriters.

The chapter starts with a literature review that exposes how most authors overlook the governments' role in negotiating loans. I propose an analytical framework that includes the governments as independent players and outlines when each side of the table—bank and government—were relatively stronger, capable of imposing their choices to the other player. I do not claim that banks were unimportant; on the contrary, depending on the circumstances they had the upper hand, but in some cases governments were on top of negotiations. The framework presented here will guide the historical analysis in the remaining of the book.

Theory and History of Sovereign Debt

The historical importance of sovereign debt is evident: It accounted for a larger share of global finance before 1914 than today, and its expansion was one of the primary drivers of the first financial globalisation.[2] Sovereign debt is also relevant to the researchers of economic theory because it entails a fundamental contract enforcement problem: In the event of default, creditors cannot rely on the law to recover their money. While lenders that hold domestically denominated public bonds may sue their government, holders of sovereign debt lack legal protection. Courts are unable to force foreign governments to commit to debt contracts.[3]

[2] According to Mauro et al. (2006, 11–19), by 1905 the stock of sovereign bonds negotiated in London totalled £4.1 billion, almost twice the size of Britain's GDP.

[3] Grossman and Van Huyck (1988, 2) assert that "sovereign debt (…) is above the law." The decision of a New York court on the Argentinean defaulted debt in the early 2010s is either an exception or the beginning of a groundbreaking trend.

The question then is why creditors lend and governments repay. The existence of the sovereign debt market is a paradox in itself. Several authors address this question, most of whom assess the creditors' side, attributing a submissive role to borrowers.

In their seminal article, Eaton and Gersovitz (1981, 290) propose that borrowers "will default if it is to their benefit." The benefit of defaulting is the suspension of payments. The higher the debt burden, the more likely the default. Most authors measure this burden as the ratio between the services due on the debt and GDP, but Tomz and Wright (2007) show that governments did default during periods of economic growth. The authors suggest that fiscal and export results produce more precise indicators of default risk. The ratio of debt services to taxes gives the fiscal burden of honouring the debt, and a similar ratio with exports indicates the burden concerning the balance of payments. This approach is historically useful, for the concept of GDP was not available in the first financial globalisation.

The cost of defaulting is the cutting off of credit after payments are suspended, as creditors are unlikely to lend to bad borrowers. This cost is persistent. Reinhart et al. (2003) argue that defaults increase the cost of borrowing in the long run, even after bad borrowers re-enter the market. Creditworthy governments face high reputational costs when they suspend payments. The better their previous payment record, the more credit they can access in normal circumstances and the more they will lose under an embargo. Hence, good borrowers are more likely to repay. Borenstein and Panizza (2010) argue that the cost of defaulting is higher when the borrower's economy is open, for lack of credit is detrimental to foreign trade, a conclusion that has been disputed by Martinez and Sandleris (2011).

According to Eaton and Gersovitz (1981), governments reach a "credit ceiling" when they increase the debt burden to the point that the benefit equals the costs of defaulting. Creditors would not lend, and governments would either default or reduce the debt burden by consolidating fiscal accounts. Tomz (2007) claims that the market rewards governments that honour their debt during bad times. Such borrowers build a reputation because they show commitment to contracts. The main concepts from Eaton and Gersovitz still apply: Contract-obeying policymakers consolidate fiscal accounts in spite of adverse shocks, preventing the debt burden from raising up to the credit ceiling.

Mitchener and Weidenmier (2010) assert that "supersanctions" enforced contracts in the nineteenth century. Creditors pressured their governments to invade borrowing countries and force defaulters to repay. Nevertheless, such "gunboat" diplomacy was an exception rather than the rule. Cain and Hopkins (2001) demonstrate that British politicians and officials were not inclined to design foreign policy to attend to the interests of bondholders. Invasions did happen, but mostly when the interests of policymakers and creditors converged, such as in the case of strategic Egypt, which became a de facto British colony following an invasion that was triggered by a default (Tunçer 2015). British troops also took the Mexican port of Veracruz and blockaded Venezuela for similar reasons. Yet such military expeditions were rare. Most debt-related military interventions happened during civil wars, which the creditors' governments used as opportunities to achieve geopolitical goals.

If the threat of invasion seldom enforced sovereign debt contracts, war and revolutions commonly caused defaults. Ozler and Tabellini (1991) argue that political instability and polarisation reduce the costs of defaulting and raise its benefits. Officials under the threat of being violently deposed will borrow as much as possible to spend in defence, improving the chances of political survival. Such short-sighted policymakers issue loans regardless the costs of repaying the debt in the rather uncertain future. In contrast, strong states can tax enough to maintain the debt burden at sustainable levels. Officials in stable countries expect to remain in office for at least a full term and to serve the state for the rest of their careers. This creates a long-term commitment to the government's capacity to borrow that raises the costs of defaulting. In short, political stability reduces the risk of default.

An influential literature highlights the role of the Gold Standard in enforcing sovereign debt contracts in politically stable countries. An increasing number of governments pegged their exchange rates to gold from the 1890s to 1914, when the cost of borrowing fell all over the world. Bordo (1995) proposes that creditors regarded the adoption of the Gold Standard as a "good housekeeping seal of approval," which prevented policymakers from printing money to finance unsound accounts. Pegged exchange rate also maintained the value of the foreign-denominated debt constant vis-à-vis the domestically denominated tax revenue, reducing the benefits of defaulting.[4] This literature implies that the governments' scope of action was limited to their own countries, where they ran economic policy and fostered political stability. The term "housekeeping" is no doubt informative.

Flandreau and Zumer (2004) tell a different story. They claim that fiscal fundamentals rather than exchange rate regimes determined the cost of servicing the sovereign debt before 1914. Terms of trade played a key role, for customs responded to a large share of tax revenue in borrowing countries. Mauro et al. (2006) also downplay the role of the Gold Standard. They found a significant correlation between variation in international liquidity and country risk.

Aceña et al. (2000, 7–9) show that external shocks repetitively forced countries in the periphery to quit the Gold Standard. Capital importers and commodity exporters, these economies were subjected to market volatility that often caused debt crises. External shocks depreciated the exchange rate, increasing the fiscal burden of servicing the foreign-denominated debt. A similar view appears in the prominent book by Marichal (1989), which emphasises how external shocks were key in conditioning "a century of debt crisis in Latin America." Pushed to the extreme, this interpretation implies that governments were passive not only in borrowing but also in managing their debt burden, which was ultimately determined by volatile external markets.

The way governments ran economic policy influenced the likelihood of default, but creditors still needed to enforce contracts by collectively penalising bad borrowers. Esteves (2007) describes how the Corporation of Foreign Bondholders played that role in the first financial globalisation. The Corporation issued annual reports that listed the governments that had suspended payments on their debt. The London Stock Exchange, to which the Corporation was affiliated, would not accept loans of countries whose debt payments were in arrears. European markets followed London in banning those borrowers from the continent. By making this blacklist public, the Corporation increased the costs of defaulting and protected the interests of creditors.

Flandreau and Flores (2009) propose that underwriters imposed an extra penalty on defaulters, for bankers tended to suspend business with bad borrowers. Such falling-outs entailed high costs when the banks

[4] See also Eichengreen and Hausmann (1999).

involved had premier status. Flandreau (2013) shows that banks often represented bondholders' committees when dealing with defaulters. This recent scholarship also focuses on the suppliers of credit, either the final creditors or the underwriters. The governments were left with the role of paying services on time to avoid being blacklisted.

Rescue Loans and the Government's Side of Sovereign Debt

A few scholars have studied the governments' side of settlements, the conversion of defaulted debt that clean bad borrowers' records. Fernandez and Rosenthal (1990) assume that governments play an active role in defining the terms of these operations. Aggarwal (1996) applies game theory to the settlements of Latin American debt from the mid-nineteenth century to the 1990s. Yet creditors are the main players in the more recent work by Kovrijnykh and Szentes (2007), who claim that lenders have incentives to reach settlements with bad borrowers in periods of economic growth. Esteves (2013) also focuses on the creditor's side when he shows that the Corporation of Foreign Bondholders was more successful in protecting the lender's interests in settlements than country-specific committees under the representation of debt underwriters.

New research shows that governments negotiated the imposition of foreign controls after settlements. Tunçer (2015) demonstrates that the Ottoman government responded to domestic pressure groups when it agreed to share policy ownership with British and French bankers in the 1870s. Instead of a simple exercise of finance imperialism, the author concludes that controls were the result of deals between high officials and foreign financiers.

This book makes the case that governments were more powerful and independent than is commonly assumed, and that happened under normal circumstances, when the debt was being honoured without financial controls. Governments were free to decide whether to commit to a single patron bank or to borrow through several different underwriters.

Based on the study of Rothschilds and Brazil, Flandreau and Flores (2012) argue that governments benefited from the association with first-class underwriters because of their capacity to attract credit. Brazil was fiscally fragile but borrowed at good terms because it conceded exclusivity to Rothschilds. The authors propose that governments were likely to commit to a single underwriter if (1) they did not have a good reputation, and (2) the candidate of patron bank was high-class. In this case, exclusive association compensated for the countries' negative status. This hypothesis is a useful starting point for the analysis of how governments dealt with underwriters, but the authors do not exploit it further, leaving a gap I address in the remaining of this chapter.

A few historical studies show that governments were independent, although they diverge from the hypothesis above. Suzuki (1994) describes that, after the conquest of Manchuria and the victory over Russia, the Japanese government negotiated with top underwriters, including Barings and Rothschilds, to issue loans at good rates. Flores (2007) studies the case of Argentina, which bargained to borrow at conditions incompatible with its deteriorating fundamentals in the 1880s. The Argentinean government did not act as one would expect from its eroding reputation and connection with Barings.

I introduce the concept of rescue loans into this discussion. Rescue loans were cheap credit facilities banks offered to governments to prevent them from defaulting on their debt during crises. These loans were cheap in proportion to the credit the rescued governments had on the secondary market; in other words, their risk premium was lower than country risk.[5] Rescue loans reduced the debt burden in bad times. It was the carrot that underwriters offered to troubled governments. Together with the stick (the suspension of businesses in the event of defaults), rescue loans aided unsound borrowers to commit to contracts. The choice of having a patron bank worked similarly to an insurance: It limited the scope for negotiation and increased borrowing costs in good times but could reduce them in bad times, depending on the bank's willingness and capacity to rescue its client.

It is important to note that rescue loans were different from settlements because they were made to avoid defaults rather than to normalise credit relations after such an event had happened. Banks could combine rescue loans with the re-contracting of the outstanding debt. Re-contracting is different from default if final creditors accept it to help the government in honouring the debt. Such an agreement may be

[5] See Chapter 1 and Data Appendix for the definition of country risk.

combined with rescue loans in a wider kind of operation I call rescue package.[6]

This book does not address the cases of Japan and Argentina, but rescue loans may explain why these countries chose not to grant monopolies to top underwriters. Japan counted upon a stream of revenue from its growing empire. The resources of Korea and Manchuria reduced the probability of debt crises and therefore the future demand for rescue loans. In Argentina, meanwhile, policymaking was decentralised among provinces, which created a moral hazard problem that is consistent with the decision of not having a patron bank. Who would pay for insurance if not a centralised state? These are possible conclusions that require future research on these specific cases, but they suggest that governments responded to incentives generated by the need and probability of rescue loans in the future.

In the absence of a world lender of last resort such as the IMF, a non-profit organisation that pursues institutional goals, private banks managed sovereign debt crises according to their market-based interests.[7] Banks had strong incentives to launch rescue loans when the costs created by eventual defaults were greater than the opportunity cost of granting cheap credit. Patron banks shared their brands with their exclusive clients, which raised the costs the former faced if the latter defaulted. For this reason, patron banks were more likely to issue rescue loans than banks that did not hold a monopoly on the governments' debt.

The incentives to rescue were proportional to the banks' status and their association with troubled borrowers. Also, premier banks had more access to credit, which enabled them to provide the large and generous rescue loans their clients needed to maintain service payments in spite of adverse shocks. Such banks were likely to have enough influence over bondholders to convince them to hold rescue bonds or even to agree upon debt re-contracting. This point takes into consideration the interaction between banks and bondholders, which Esteves (2013) addresses and is on purpose overlooked in this book. By assuming that premier banks had a greater capacity to arrange the support of final creditors in rescuing packages, I can focus on this book's topic: The relations between governments and banks.

[6]The Greek haircuts of the early 2010s were part of a rescue package rather than a default, for the creditors accepted to reduce the principal of the debt.

[7]See Roch and Uhlig (2016) for recent work on the role of the IMF.

Summing up, governments that had developed exclusive association with high-class banks were more likely to be rescued than those that had issued loans through many second-rank underwriters.

It is reasonable to assume that banks were more willing to grant rescue loans during liquidity rather than structural crises. They would not grant cheap credit forever. What is more, cyclical crises created business opportunities. Rescue loans could become profitable if the price of bonds eventually increased once the crisis was over. The more the bankers expected such an event, the greater their incentives to launch rescue loans. Besides protecting reputation, underwriters could make money by helping illiquid governments.

A regime change that permanently deteriorates accounts or a loss of territory that shrinks the tax base structurally compromises fiscal sustainability. Liquidity crises, on the other hand, were often associated with fluctuations in export prices and world liquidity. Such external shocks increased the risk of default until the markets for goods and capital bounced back.[8] Nevertheless, patron banks still rescued governments that fought wars and revolutions. Such cases were likely when the cost of not acting was exceedingly high, and the bankers believed that the country had substantial chances of being pacified. Rothschilds rescued Brazil in the turbulent 1890s. The bank funded the government in its effort to pacify the new republic. Banks treated Mexico differently during the Revolution, during which the government suspended debt payments, and the state subsequently collapsed.

These contrasting events influenced the development of Brazil and Mexico as nation states. Brazil is still a republic and, as I write, Mexico's president belongs to the Institutional Revolutionary Party (PRI), which emerged from the war against the counter-revolutionary administration that failed to borrow cheaply. If rescue loans (and the lack of) played a role in defining these countries' long-term political history, these operations probably shaped the relations between these governments and the underwriters of their debt in the first financial globalisation.

[8]In a historically distant although related case, Drelichman and Voth (2011) show that Genovese bankers provided credit to the Spanish Empire under Philip II when the sovereign lacked funds to honour the debt.

The Government's Choice: Patron Banking or Competition

Patron banking increased the chances of rescue loans during crises. This expectation created incentives for governments to grant exclusivity to underwriters, and thus complements Flandreau and Flores' "brand" argument, according to which patron banks could improve their borrowers' reputation. In addition to that, the association with a single bank also helped governments in establishing business connections with foreign companies that operated in sectors such as railways, domestic banking, foreign trade and the construction of public works. As will be detailed in this book, patron banks often connected their clients with such companies. In some cases, the underwriters of sovereign debt also acted in these unrelated sectors.[9] Rescue loans and business connections—in addition to "brands"—explained the reasons why some governments decided to have patron banks.

Patron banks spawned positive payoffs regardless of their status, but first-class banks generated more significant gains than mediocre contenders. British premier underwriters had a great capacity of attracting the credit necessary in large and cheap rescue loans. That was less the case with emerging banks based in the European continent and the USA. The same applies to business connections: Premier bankers had access to premier contractors, traders and financiers, and thus could help their clients to cut top deals. The choice of having a patron bank depended on the comparison between these benefits and the opportunity cost of granting exclusivity—not being able to negotiate loans. This cost was crucial. The fact that many governments chose not to be associated with a single underwriter confirms that their capacity to negotiate mattered.

In this book, I explore the corollary of Flandreau and Flores' hypothesis exposed in the previous section: Assuming that first-class banks were not an option, would governments of worthy status promote competition among second-class underwriters to improve credit conditions or would they grant a monopoly to benefit from patron banking? The authors admit that they "neglect this property" (Flandreau and Flores 2009, 13).

[9] See Vizcarra (2009) for the case of Peru.

The Porfirian government corresponded to such a case. Mexico was a previous serial defaulter that converted its old debt in a successful settlement and ran sound policies in a benign conjuncture of growth and stability. Its bonds attracted final creditors, but premier banks would still not underwrite them. With high-class banks out of reach, the officials of the Porfiriato had to decide whether to grant exclusivity to or to negotiate loans with mediocre underwriters. The choice of having a second-class patron bank increased the chances of arranging rescue loans and of cutting deals not directly related to sovereign debt. But these payoffs were lower than the opportunity cost of not negotiating loans. Thus, the Mexican government used its newly acquired reputation to foster competition among banks.

The comparison with Brazil is enlightening. The Brazilian government decided to be Rothschilds' most faithful client and later received rescue loans that prevented it from defaulting. It is noteworthy that second-class banks repeatedly tried to become Mexico's patron banks, but Díaz and his officials consistently declined the offers. We do not know if they would have acted differently had Rothschilds been an option. But the evidence analysed in this book shows that, by not granting exclusivity, the Mexican government successfully negotiated favourable loans with many banks. That was a good *ex-ante* strategy in the 1900s, during the apogee of the Porfiriato, when no one anticipated the crisis that would hit the country in the following decade. By the time Mexico hit the credit ceiling during the Revolution, however, the government lacked a patron bank that would meet its urgent need of credit.

The cases of Brazil and Mexico support Flandreau and Flores' hypothesis and its corollary, respectively. The Brazilian government was a second-class borrower that granted exclusivity to benefit from the brand of a premier bank. The Mexican government refused to have a patron bank because it was building a reputation but could only access unprestigious banks. This interpretation is consistent with the concept of rescue loan. A premier underwriter, Rothschilds had much at stake in terms of reputation and thus was more likely to rescue its client than the mediocre banks that underwrote Mexican debt.

Nevertheless, the study of these historical cases suggests three additional features that seem to have influenced the way these governments related to banks. Firstly, Brazil did not choose to have a patron bank only because that increased its status as a borrower. By appointing Rothschilds as its financial agent, the government opened a range of business connections in London. The contract that united the government and the bank explicitly stated that the latter represented the former in the purchases of goods in Europe.[10] Rothschilds routinely received queries from British companies interested in Brazil, most of which contacted the government through the bank.[11]

Secondly, the suspension of credit monopolies did not involve prohibitive costs, and governments had incentives of doing so once they had built a good reputation. Brazil borrowed in Paris through banks other than Rothschilds in the prosperous late 1900s and early 1910s. That did not trigger penalties; the government maintained its business with its former patron bank, borrowing at increasingly cheaper rates. Rothschilds' brand was still important, but not nearly as much as in had been six decades before, when the market was less competitive, information was more imperfect, and Brazil was not an established borrower. The government's incentives to grant exclusivity were circumstantial, and monopolies did not last indefinitely.

Finally, non-economic features of these countries also conditioned their governments' choices. Several world powers invaded Mexico before the rise of Díaz, so that the maintenance of independence and sovereignty legitimised his regime. Those in charge of debt negotiations followed a nationalistic ideology when dealing with foreign bankers. It is possible that Mexico would have declined a patron banking offer even if it came from Rothschilds. The Brazilian Empire, in contrast, was Latin America's most stable regime (followed by Chile, which for one reason or another also adopted Rothschilds as a patron bank). The association with Rothschilds was not such a contentious issue as it would have been in Porfirian Mexico. Everything equal, Mexico was less prone to have a patron bank than Brazil.

Analytical Framework

The power of the Brazilian and Mexican governments relative to their debt underwriters depended on the banks' exposure to their client in the case of Brazil and on the government's recently established reputation in the case of Mexico. On the banks' side, Rothschilds' premier status made it strong in the 1850s, when Brazil approved a deal that prevented it

[10] *RA* XI/65/000/401.

[11] *RA* contains piles of letters from British investors and contractors interested in Brazil, who asked the bankers for information and intermediation.

from negotiating loans with other underwriters. However, exposure and status empowered the government during the troublesome 1890s and 1910s. Brazil would have had a slimmer chance of accessing cheap credit had it been associated with a less prestigious bank. That was the case of Mexico, which failed to arrange a rescue loan during the Revolution. These case studies provide insights for the analysis of the balance of power between governments and bankers in several different set-ups of the first financial globalisation.

Creditworthy governments were powerful vis-à-vis banks. Their debt was unlikely to go into default, so underwriting it involved little reputational risk. Furthermore, underwriters could sell their bonds at a high price on the secondary market, raising the prospect of profits. Such governments could negotiate good deals every time they issued a new loan. The more they bargained, the higher the price at which they sold their debt to the underwriters and the lower the commission they paid. Negotiation raised the government's revenue and squeezed the banks' profit.

The power of banks vis-à-vis governments depended on their status in the hierarchy among underwriters. Status was directly proportional to the time the banks had operated on the market and inversely related to the number of defaults on the bonds they had underwritten. Exposure also determined the power of banks. A premier bank could become weak vis-à-vis its client if they had developed a solid association. Default would significantly impact the bank's status, which created leverage for the government to pressure for rescue loans. Exposure was high when the underwriter had been the government's patron bank for a long time. Although to a lesser extent, exposure was still significant when banks and governments were not so firmly connected but had a significant degree of association. A default would always deteriorate the underwriter's status. Banks were also exposed to governments when they held a considerable amount of their debt. Yet financial exposure did not play a significant role in the cases analysed in this book.

Figure 2.1 illustrates an extreme case in which the government is weak and the bank strong. The government has a poor debt record, while political instability reduces the costs of default and increases its benefits. The government is near or at the credit ceiling. All this means that it is in a weak position to negotiate borrowing terms and is likely to accept whatever the bank offers. The bank is a premier underwriter that has not done business with that government. It will have incentives to avoid

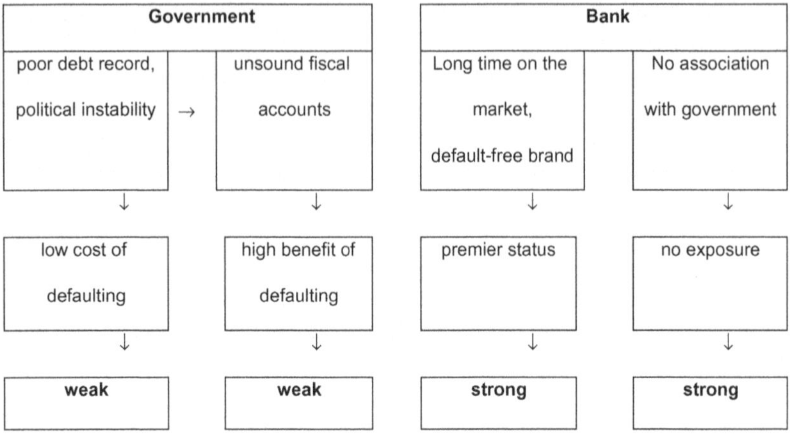

Fig. 2.1 Weak government, strong bank

the government and no reason to issue a rescue loan. This is not a case for patron banking. If the bank proposes exclusive association, the government will have incentives to free ride on its credit umbrella in the likely event of a debt crisis. Underwriters are not inclined to become the patron bank of unsound borrowers, and this is more the case the higher the banks' status, for high-class underwriters are more likely to grant rescue loans. It is striking that the case in which the bank is the strongest and the government is the weakest is improbable.

Figure 2.2 shows the opposite extreme of a strong government but a weak bank. The government has a good record, and debt burden is way below the credit ceiling, so it is a creditworthy borrower that will attract several competing banks. The government is likely to use its relative power to negotiate favourable terms. Given its second-rank reputation, the bank will only have a chance to underwrite the government's debt if it offers a good deal, as the government could always bargain for better conditions with other banks. Low commission and high issuing price will keep the bank's profitability low and the government's revenue high. Finally, the bank's exposure creates incentives for rescuing the government if a debt crisis makes its payment capacity deteriorate.

Ironically, the government in Fig. 2.2 is the most attractive for patron banking, but it is the most unlikely to grant exclusivity. Yet this

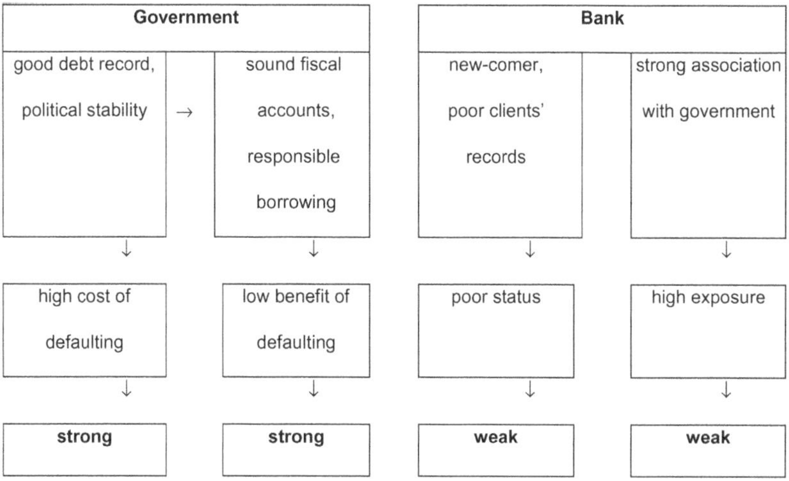

Fig. 2.2 Strong government, weak bank

does not mean that governments and banks are always unlikely to agree upon exclusive deals. The cases depicted above are extreme, and many possible combinations lay in the middle. Risk-averse governments may grant a monopoly on their debt as an insurance even if their reputation is good. Risk-neutrals may accept patron banking to improve their status and profit from business connections, although this specific association is likely to finish if the borrowers become high class.

Rothschilds was similar to the premier bank in Fig. 2.1. During the 1850s, Brazil was a better borrower than the government in that figure, but it was still weak in relation to its recently appointed patron bank. The balance would change in favour of the government as the bank underwrote a large number of loans, improving Brazil's reputation and increasing Rothschilds' exposure. Mexico resembled the government in Fig. 2.1 before the rise of Porfirio Díaz, but became more similar to the creditworthy borrower of Fig. 2.2 as the Porfirian government established a reputation. Officials refused to grant exclusivity so that they could negotiate with different banks. This book analyses the historical reasons behind these two different outcomes—association with a patron bank and negotiation with many banks.

Matters are more complex when a premier bank is exposed to a government that hits the credit ceiling, a case Fig. 2.3 illustrates. The debt crisis reduces the government's capacity to attract other banks, but it also enables officials to threaten a default to make the bank grant a rescue loan. Given its reputation and exposure, the bank has little option but to comply.

The horizontal arrow from "credit ceiling" on the government's side and the vertical arrows from "premier status" and "high exposure" on the bank's side indicate that the combination of these three factors weakens the bank vis-à-vis the government. This outcome is less likely when banks are second-class, for some bad bonds would have a smaller effect in their status. A mediocre underwriter would have had fewer incentives than Rothschilds to rescue Brazil. Rothschilds' premier reputation made it weaker, not stronger, when its exclusive client hit the credit ceiling. Exposure and status created room for free riding: the Brazilian officials counted on rescue loans and the government faced a relatively low cost when it deteriorated fiscal accounts to attend political demands during the 1890s. The case of Brazil was more complex than that of Mexico, which had the leverage to negotiate but not to free ride on the underwriters of its debt.

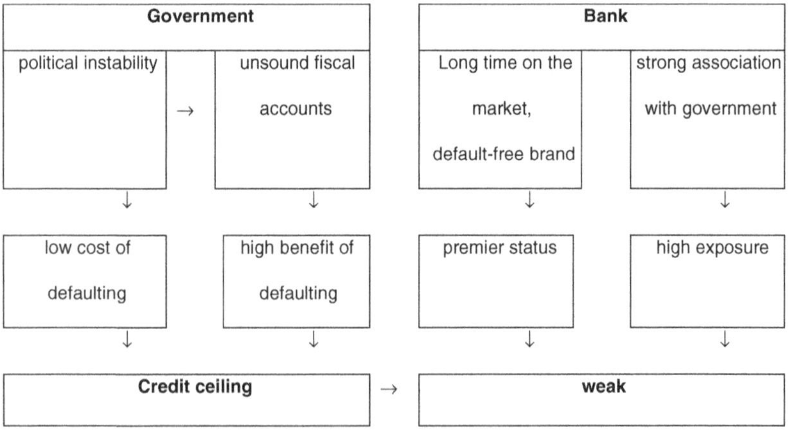

Fig. 2.3 Government in crisis, exposed premier bank

Conclusion

Governments were independent decision-makers in the sovereign debt market of the first financial globalisation. They decided whether to grant exclusivity to a single patron bank or to negotiate with competing banks to reduce borrowing costs. Both options entailed positive and negative payoffs. Patron banks could raise the governments' reputation and create business connections. Exclusivity also increased the chances that banks would grant cheap rescue loans in times of crisis to prevent their clients from defaulting. By agreeing on exclusivity, however, governments would not bargain for better deals with other underwriters. The outcomes of lending negotiations depended on the relative power of governments and banks. Both players were strong when they counted with good reputation among the public. Yet premier banks became weak when they were exposed to governments that faced debt crises, for these troubled clients could threaten to default to pressure for the issuing of rescue loans.

References

Archival Sources

RA Rothschilds Archive, London.
Correspondence, XI.

Secondary Sources

Acеña, Pablo Martin, and Jaime Reis, eds. 2000. *Monetary Standards in the Periphery: Paper, Silver and Gold, 1854–1933*. New York: Palgrave Macmillan.

Aggarwal, Vinod K. 1996. *Debt Games: Strategic Interaction in International Debt Rescheduling*. Cambridge: Cambridge University Press.

Bordo, Michael D. 1995. "The Gold Standard as a 'Good Housekeeping Seal of Approval'." Working Paper 5340. National Bureau of Economic Research.

Borensztein, Eduardo, and Ugo Panizza. 2010. "Do Sovereign Defaults Hurt Exporters?" *Open Economies Review* 21 (3):393–412.

Cain, P. J., and A. G. Hopkins. 2001. *British Imperialism: 1688–2000*. London: Routledge.

Drelichman, Mauricio, and Hans-Joachim Voth. 2011. "Lending to the Borrower from Hell: Debt and Default in the Age of Philip II." *Economic Journal* 121 (557):1205–27.

Eaton, Jonathan, and Mark Gersovitz. 1981. "Debt with Potential Repudiation: Theoretical and Empirical Analysis." *The Review of Economic Studies* 48 (2):289–309.

Eichengreen, Barry, and Ricardo Hausmann. 1999. "Exchange Rates and Financial Fragility." Working Paper 7418. National Bureau of Economic Research.

Esteves, Rui P. 2007. "Quis Custodiet Quem? Sovereign Debt and Bondholders' Protection Before 1914." Economics Series Working Papers 323. University of Oxford, Department of Economics.

———. 2013. "The Bondholder, the Sovereign, and the Banker: Sovereign Debt and Bondholders' Protection before 1914." *European Review of Economic History* 17 (4):389–407.

Fernandez, Raquel, and Robert W. Rosenthal. 1990. "Strategic Models of Sovereign-Debt Renegotiations." *The Review of Economic Studies* 57 (3):331–49.

Flandreau, Marc. 2013. "Sovereign States, Bondholders Committees, and the London Stock Exchange in the Nineteenth Century (1827–68): New Facts and Old Fictions." *Oxford Review of Economic Policy* 29 (4):668–96.

Flandreau, Marc, and Juan H. Flores. 2009. "Bonds and Brands: Foundations of Sovereign Debt Markets, 1820–1830." *The Journal of Economic History* 69 (3):646–84.

———. 2012. "Bondholders Versus Bond-Sellers? Investment Banks and Conditionality Lending in the London Market for Foreign Government Debt, 1815–1913." *European Review of Economic History* 16 (4):356–83.

Flandreau, Marc, and Frédéric Zumer. 2004. *The Making of Global Finance 1880–1913.* Paris: OECD.

Flores, Juan H. 2007. "Lending Booms, Underwriting and Competition: The Baring Crisis Revisited." IFCS Working Papers in Economic History 07-01.

Grossman, Herschel I., and John B. Van Huyck. 1988. "Sovereign Debt as a Contingent Claim: Excusable Default, Repudiation, and Reputation." *The American Economic Review* 78 (5):1088–97.

Kovrijnykh, Natalia, and Balázs Szentes. 2007. "Equilibrium Default Cycles." *Journal of Political Economy* 115 (3):403–46.

Marichal, Carlos. 1989. *A Century of Debt Crises in Latin America: From Independence to the Great Depression, 1820–1930.* Princeton: Princeton University Press.

Martinez, José V., and Guido Sandleris. 2011. "Is It Punishment? Sovereign Defaults and the Decline in Trade." *Journal of International Money and Finance* 30 (6):909–30.

Mauro, Paolo, Nathan Sussman, and Yishay Yafeh. 2006. *Emerging Markets and Financial Globalization: Sovereign Bond Spreads in 1870–1913 and Today.* Oxford: Oxford University Press.

Mitchener, Kris J., and Marc D. Weidenmier. 2010. "Supersanctions and Sovereign Debt Repayment." *Journal of International Money and Finance* 29 (1):19–36.

Ozler, Sule, and Guido Tabellini. 1991. "External Debt and Political Instability." CEPR Discussion Papers 582.

Reinhart, Carmen M., Kenneth S. Rogoff, and Miguel A. Savastano. 2003. "Debt Intolerance." *Brookings Papers on Economic Activity* 2003 (1):1–74.

Roch, Francisco, and Harald Uhlig. 2016. *The Dynamics of Sovereign Debt Crises and Bailouts*. Washington, DC: International Monetary Fund.

Suzuki, Toshio. 1994. *Japanese Government Loan Issues on the London Capital Market, 1870–1913*. London: Athlone Press.

Tomz, Michael. 2007. *Reputation and International Cooperation: Sovereign Debt Across Three Centuries*. Princeton: Princeton University Press.

Tomz, Michael, and Mark L. J. Wright. 2007. "Do Countries Default in 'Bad Times'?" *Journal of the European Economic Association* 5 (2–3):352–60

Tunçer, Ali C. 2015. *Sovereign Debt and International Financial Control: The Middle East and the Balkans, 1870–1914*. London: Palgrave Macmillan.

Vizcarra, Catalina. 2009. "Guano, Credible Commitments, and Sovereign Debt Repayment in Nineteenth-Century Peru." *The Journal of Economic History* 69 (2):358–87.

PART II

Brazil versus Rothschilds

CHAPTER 3

Rothschilds' Tropical Empire: Brazil, 1822–1889

Brazil's sovereign debt was a matter of Rothschilds *par excellence*. The bank participated in the transfer of a Portuguese debt to the newly independent Brazilian Empire in an agreement that allowed the new country to establish diplomatic relations with Britain. It also underwrote two loans in the 1820s. But it was in the 1850s that relations intensified: The government appointed Rothschilds as the Empire's financial agent in Europe and granted a monopoly on its debt, which lasted until 1908.

This chapter provides background for the other chapters of Part II. It reviews the relations between Rothschilds and Brazil during the period in which the country was a monarchy, between 1822 and 1889. It assesses the relative power between bank and government and its evolution over time. The Brazilian Empire granted exclusivity to Rothschilds in 1855, when the bank was already first-class and the government had a mediocre reputation. The government would not have been able to borrow to the extent and at the rate it did if it was not for Rothschilds. Association improved the country's status as a borrower, and thus the granting of a monopoly on the sovereign debt was a relatively small price to be paid.

For Rothschilds, exclusivity guaranteed that it would profit from high commission on future loans, a correct interpretation given Brazil's political stability and prospect for growth. The bank had the upper hand over the government. Relations intensified thereafter. The government borrowed extensively to finance public works and to convert the domestic debt issued during the Paraguayan War, South America's largest conflict. By 1889, Brazil was Rothschilds' second most important client, behind

L. Weller, *Sovereign Debt Crises and Negotiations in Brazil and Mexico, 1888-1914*, https://doi.org/10.1007/978-3-319-73633-4_3

only Russia. An eventual default would have had terrible consequences to the house's reputation as an underwriter. That empowered the government, providing it with leverage to free ride on the bank during the debt crisis of the 1890s, which is the topic of Chapter 4.

Rothschilds Picks a Tropical Empire

The end of the Napoleonic Wars set the stage for the expansion of global finance. Peace liberated British capital to fund the newly independent states that appeared in Latin America and Europe in the post-war. A series of defaults followed the debt boom. Most of the banks in charge of underwriting the debt of foreign countries closed their doors. Together with Barings, Rothschilds was the only house that survived the 1820s without underwriting bad loans (Flandreau and Flores 2009).

Rothschilds was the bank of European Empires. Between 1818 and 1824, it underwrote loans of Prussian, Russia, and Austria, apart from Britain and France. The only exception was Brazil. The bankers approached that new Latin American country in 1823, a year after its independence from Portugal. Rothschilds drafted the contract for what would have been the first Brazilian loan, in partnership with Samuel Phillips, also from London. Nathan Rothschild made the loan conditional on the establishment of diplomatic relations between the new country and Britain, which would only happen if Portugal accepted independence.[1] Portugal and Britain recognised Brazil as a sovereign state in 1825 through an arrangement in which Rothschilds was directly involved. The deal involved the transfer of £1.4 million in debt from Portugal to Brazil, which Rothschilds intermediated under the supervision of the British government (Rodrigues and Seitenfus 1995, 135).

Nevertheless, the Brazilian government borrowed abroad in 1824, before establishing diplomatic relations with Portugal and Britain. Instead of Rothschilds, three other London banks—Bazenth, Farqhuar, Crawford & Co.; Fletcher, Alexander & Co.; and Thomas Wilson & Co.—launched the loan. These houses closed their doors a few months later, amid the wave of defaults that hit the market that year, after having issued only one-third of the bonds. Rothschilds underwrote the remainder of the

[1] *RA* XI/38/215A.

operation in 1825, while it was negotiating the transfer of the Portuguese debt.

Why did Rothschilds decide to associate itself with Brazil, a faraway former colony of the decadent Portuguese Empire? A possible answer is the fact that the new country was a monarchy. The founder of the Brazilian Empire was Dom Pedro I, the son of the Portuguese king Dom João VI. Both noblemen moved to Rio de Janeiro together with the entire court in 1808, running away from Napoleon's troops. Dom João returned to Lisbon in 1821 to prevent a revolution in Porto from toppling the monarchy. He left his son in Brazil, who proclaimed independence the following year. The arrangement was a family matter: Dom Pedro was the first in line to the Portuguese throne, and his reign in Brazil made a future Luso-Brazilian reunification likely.

The foundation of the Brazilian Empire created a peculiar situation in which the Portuguese Dom Pedro proclaimed independence from his home-nation Portugal. Dom Pedro belonged to the royal houses of Orleans e Bragança and Hapsburg, which legitimised his rule. The new country's flag was green and yellow, these houses' respective colours. Dawson (1990, 93) affirms that such peculiarity attracted Rothschilds. The issuing of Brazilian bonds allowed the bank to participate in the Latin American debt boom of the 1820s without upsetting its clients of the Holy Alliance—Austria, Russia and Prussia opposed the division of the Spanish colonies into independent republics.

Brazil was also singular in economic and institutional terms. Before independence, it responded for most of the wealth, territory and population of the Portuguese Empire. It was not by chance that Rio de Janeiro hosted the Portuguese court during the Napoleonic Wars (Cardoso and Linhares 2000). The process that led to independence was also exceptional. While long civil wars wobbled Spanish America, Dom Pedro's forces only fought isolated battles in Salvador, Belém and São Luís, cities that were particularly connected to Portugal. Some member of the Portuguese courts stayed in Rio de Janeiro, including judges and clerks who helped to maintain law and order and to raise taxes (Bethell 1985). Independence was less disruptive than in the rest of Latin America, which made Brazil a better borrower than its neighbours (Marichal 1989, 35; Taylor 2003, 5).

The Brazilian Empire was an institutionally stable and centralised parliamentary monarchy. It had a single constitution from 1824 to 1891, which makes it the most persistent in the country's history. The document created the *Poder Moderador* (Moderating Power), which was entitled to "coordinate" the Executive, Legislative and Judiciary. A Council of State and the emperor composed the Moderating Power, but in practice the latter had a great influence over the other state branches. The emperor had the prerogative to appoint the twelve members of the Council of State and to nominate senators. The Council of State selected provincial presidents (the equivalent of governors) and had the power to dissolve the ministerial cabinet, which composed the Executive Branch and was entitled to appoint judges across the country (Carvalho 1988, 107).

The Parliament was, in theory, independent from the emperor. Yet he influenced congressmen because of his prerogative to nominate ministers and to form cabinets. Nevertheless, the Legislative branch had a say on the budget and used that power to guarantee that the government would honour its debt. The Parliament represented the interests of the domestic creditors of the state, who either had a sit in the house or connections with its members (Graham 1977). According to Summerhill (2015), the Legislative limited the Executive Branch, reducing default risk and enabling the government to borrow extensively at home. Summerhill points out that the Parliament also protected the rights of foreign creditors. A default on the sovereign debt would have reduced the credit in London, putting pressure on the budget and increasing the risk of default domestically.

There is little room for doubt that its stable institutions made the Brazilian Empire a better borrower than most Latin American republics. That must have played a role in shaping Nathan Rothschilds' decision of doing business with the Empire. Yet one should not downplay the clashes between Dom Pedro and the Parliament. Disputes over the balance of power polarised national politics. The Portuguese-born elite of Rio de Janeiro and leaders linked to Dom Pedro were in favour a centralised state. Their opponents were Brazilian-born who composed a parliamentary majority (Jeffrey 2006, 42).

The Parliament approved a first draft of the constitution in 1823. The document limited the powers of the emperor, who in response vetoed the draft and dissolved the assembly. Dom Pedro and his closest collaborators wrote the final version of the constitution, which a new Parliament ratified under intense pressure from the Crown (Monteiro 2000, 136–37). Dom Pedro won the constitutional quarrel, but most congressmen never recognised the 1825 agreement with Portugal, which turned the Portuguese debt into a delicate issue.

Brazil's First Crisis and Rescue Loan

The Brazilian Empire became financially and politically unstable during the Cisplatine War, which it fought from 1825 to 1828 against Buenos Aires and local rebels in the province that is today Uruguay. The conflict ended when Britain imposed the creation of Uruguay as a buffer state (Carneiro 1983). This outcome had terrible consequences for Dom Pedro's rule. His troops failed to secure access to the Plata river, which would have raised customs collection and eventually paid for the campaign. Military expenditure increased up to the point that the Empire ran its most unsound accounts ever in 1826. Expenditure surpassed tax revenue in 215% (IBGE 1990, 57–571, 616–18). By 1826, the government had spent the entire 1824–1825 loan and lacked the funds in London to pay foreign bondholders (Bouças 1955, 117).

The state-owned Banco do Brasil played a key role in state finance during the Cisplatine War (Mettenheim 2015, 32–34). It printed a large amount of notes vis-à-vis its reduced bullion reserves so that the government could pay for the conflict. A financial crisis culminated with a run on Banco do Brasil, which closed its doors in 1829 (Peláez and Suzigan 1981, 55–56). The government also minted copper coins that, together with the Banco do Brasil's notes, depreciated the exchange rate by 52% during the Cisplatine War (IBGE 1990, 522–23). The weak *mil-réis* raised the value of the sovereign debt (denominated in British pounds) to over three times tax revenue.[2]

Rothschilds arranged a loan in 1829 in partnership with Thomas Wilson. The operation involved £769,200, the equivalent of 13% of the Brazilian sovereign debt (Bouças 1955).[3] The government sold the bonds to them at 52% of face value, way below the average of 82% at which it had issued the 1824–1825 loan. The risk premium was 6.79%, which makes the 1829 loan the most expensive of the monarchic period.[4] Yet the operation was still a rescue loan because the London market was virtually closed to new Latin American debt. Brazil would not have been able to borrow without Rothschilds.

[2] Calculated from Bouças (1955, 120) and IBGE (1990, 57–571, 616–18).

[3] Ibid.

[4] Calculated from Bouças (1955) and *The Investor's Monthly Manual*. See Table 1.1.

The 1829 loan covered payments that Rothschilds had made on behalf of the government and financed the services due in the following years (Summerhill 2015, 57). Brazil would have probably joined the 1820s wave of defaults without that operation. Rothschilds held the bonds until market conditions improved and sold them at a margin (Flandreau and Flores 2009, 673). Brazil had become an important client by then. After the launching of the loan, the Brazilian debt accounted for 11% of all the sovereign bonds Rothschilds had underwritten so far, close to the levels of Prussia and Russia (Ayers 1905).[5]

Political conditions deteriorated during the 1830s and 1840s, when Rothschilds did not underwrite Brazilian loans. Riots forced Dom Pedro to depart in exile in 1831, but his six-year-old son Dom Pedro II stayed. Regents in favour of political decentralisation ruled the country until the prince was old enough to become emperor. Meanwhile, local groups fought civil wars across the country, disputing the power handed to regional authorities (Basile 2000, 225). The regents reduced the size of the Army, which only intervened in the Farrapos War (1835–1845), a major conflict that threatened the integrity of the national territory in Brazil's south. Security became overall a measure of informal militias loyal to local leader.

Decentralisation shrunk the imperial budget and strengthened fiscal accounts, reducing the pressure on monetary emission. The *mil-réis* stopped depreciating, and the services due on the sovereign debt remained stable vis-à-vis tax revenue. Brazil borrowed £1.14 in London in two small loans underwritten by Samuel Phillips and Isaac Lyon Goldsmid in 1839 and 1843, respectively. Accounts were not as unsound as in the 1820s, and the government was able to borrow domestically to finance the deficit.[6]

The Return of Rothschilds

Rothschilds resumed doing business with Brazil in the 1850s. It underwrote seven loans for £18.4 million between 1852 and 1865, more than twice the amount the government had borrowed in London in the previous three decades. Rothschilds became the government's financial agent

[5] If one does not consider Britain, which responded to 46%, the Brazilian share is 20%, behind Prussia and Russia, with 28% and 22%, respectively.

[6] See Summerhill (2015, 93) for more on the domestic debt.

in Europe. Signed in 1855, the agreement provided the bank with exclusivity on sovereign debt issuing, beginning a monopoly that lasted for five decades.

The bank's managers played the role of state advisors, regularly informing policymakers on the condition of the debt market in London and political developments in Europe. British investors also sought guidance from Rothschilds when investing in the country. The Rothschild Archive holds a vast collection of correspondence between the house and the government, as well as with British companies that approached the bankers to get information on Brazil and to access Brazilian officials. The 1855 contract obliged the government to carry out purchases of equipment for public works and transportation in Europe through the bank, which was constantly connecting high officials with contractors, traders and financiers in London.[7]

The new loans were substantially cheaper. While Brazil borrowed at an average risk premium of 3.5% during the First Reign and the Regency, it did so at 1.9% between 1850 and 1863, the year of the last loan issued before the Paraguayan war. Running Bay-Perron tests on Brazilian risk, Summerhill found structural breaks in 1850, which indicate that the cost of credit fell crucially in that year. Most of the funds borrowed in the 1850s converted older and more expensive bonds. That included the Portuguese debt, which had the potential of compromising Brazil's clean record (Bouças 1955, 146–47). That obligation had been part of a diplomatic dispute between both countries when Dom Pedro I returned to Portugal to combat his brother Dom Miguel. The Brazilian government did not recognise Dom Miguel's rule and refused to pay interests to Portugal, depositing the services due in a third-party account in London (Summerhill, 2017).

Credit costs fell in a period of intense institutional changes in Brazil. The coronation of Dom Pedro II in 1841 marked the beginning of the Second Reign, which lasted for forty-eight years without any disruption. The fifteen-year-old emperor had the support of most members of the two political parties that emerged in Parliament during the Regency: The Liberal and the Conservative. However, a minority of the liberals opposed the early coronation of Dom Pedro II. They launched a revolt in the states of São Paulo and Minas Gerais, but the Crown quickly crushed the rebellion (Jeffrey 2006, 103).

[7]The contract establishing Rothschilds as the Brazilian agent is in that collection: *RA* XI/65/000/401. Shaw (2005) provides a useful general guide.

The suppression of the liberal opposition was a victory for the conservative cabinet that served in office at the time. Yet Dom Pedro II invited the Liberal Party to form a new cabinet in 1844, playing the role of moderator for the first time. The alternation of parties in power was crucial to consolidate the imperial state. It fostered the political system of conciliation that avoided political polarisation and maintained stability (Carvalho 1988, 17). The liberal cabinet increased tariffs on imports, which balanced fiscal accounts (Bethell 1985, 90). The exchange rate appreciated to 27 *mil-réis* per pence, which the government established as a legal party denominated as "golden *mil-réis.*" Often used in official documents, golden coexisted with paper *mil-réis*. The difference between the two currencies was small for most of the 1850s, when the exchange rate was stable, but was going to increase greatly in the following decades (Villela 2001, 85).

The Conservative Party returned to office and abolished the slave trade in 1850. Brazilians had been intermediating the commerce of captives from Africa since colonial times. Britain forced Dom Pedro I to make it illegal, but traders continued to bring slaves to the Americas, including to the Caribbean and the Plata bay. High profits prevented the government from repressing that business in spite of the Royal Navy, which often seized vessels at high sea. The number of voyages increased steeply in the 1830s and 1840s, when over 700 thousand African captives arrived in Brazil (Alencastro 2000). British ships eventually entered Brazilian waters to make the authorities enforce the prohibition. The end of the slave trade liberated capital to the rest of the economy (Peláez and Suzigan 1981). The government also implemented a commercial code in 1850, which enabled the creation of joint stock companies (Minguzzi 1974). Together with the end of the slave trade, the commercial code conditioned the rise in investment. For the first time, the Empire saw some economic dynamism.

South American politics pacified after the fall of Juan Manuel Rosas in 1952. Rosas ruled Buenos Aires for most of the previous three decades. He attempted to unite the region that had once been the Viceroyalty of the Río de la Plata, which included today's Argentina and Uruguay. Rosas was in a permanent state of war with countryside leaders, especially in Entre Ríos, a province that borders Brazil and Uruguay. The Brazilian Empire formed an alliance against Rosas that included the troops of Justo José de Urquiza, the leader of Entre Ríos, and the Blanco Party in Uruguay. The coalition defeated Rosas, who went into exile, reducing the threat of wars in the Southern Cone (Lynch 2001). Summerhill (2015) asserts that the demise of Rosas was the key event behind the decrease in borrowing costs in Brazil.

While Brazil and the Southern Cone pacified, coffee production expanded from the Rio de Janeiro state to the more fertile plains of São Paulo. Foreign companies and the government started to build a network of railways from the coffee region to the port cities of Santos and Rio de Janeiro (Topik, 43–46). Exports increased on average by 6% per year in the 1850s, against only 2% between 1822 and 1849. Trade continued to grow until the end of the monarchy, although at a slower pace—exports expanded annually by 4% between 1850 and 1889. Coffee was the economic engine of the Second Reign. By 1889, that staple responded to 79% of national exports (IBGE 1990, 569, 616).

Customs was the most important source of fiscal revenue, and thus the coffee boom raised taxation. Measured in British pounds, the Crown's tax revenue grew by 17% annually between the 1850s and the 1880s. Together with political stabilisation and the development of the coffee sector, strong macroeconomic fundamentals played a role in improving credit conditions. That was going to change as Brazil fought the largest war in South American history in the 1860s.

Paraguayan War and Debt Boom

Brazil, Argentina and Uruguay fought the Paraguayan War between 1864 and 1870. The campaign was a reaction against the expansionist policies of Solano López, who ran a militarised dictatorship in landlocked Paraguay. Brazil responded for most of the alliance's forces, which killed the majority of the male Paraguayan population before defeating López.

Rothschilds was openly against the war. The bankers sent a letter to Parliament condemning Brazil's decision to combat Paraguay, but the bank underwrote the largest Brazilian loan to that date in 1865, at the beginning of hostilities.[8] The loan was for £6.96 million, nearly half of Brazil's sovereign debt stock. The risk premium was higher than the previous lending: 3.77%.[9] It is noteworthy, however, that the government

[8] *RA* Rothschilds to Brazilian Government, 15 August 1865, XI/142/1864–1868.

[9] Calculated from Bolças (1955) and *The Investor's Monthly Manual.*

was able to issue such a large credit facility in spite of Rothschilds' opposition to the conflict.

The war was so costly that the 1865 loan financed only 8% of Brazil's campaign, which Paláez and Suzigan (1981, 142) estimate in £87 million. Tax revenue accounted for 43% of the campaign, by far the largest share. Monetary emission responded to 17% and the domestic debt to 32%. Brazil was already a fiscal state, able to increase taxation and borrow domestically in *mil-réis*. But the war had pronounced negative macroeconomic consequences. The government ran a fiscal deficit that corresponded to 71% of tax revenue and the exchange rate depreciated by 34% during the conflict (IBGE 1990, 591, 616–18).

Slaves composed a significant share of Brazil's troops, an anomaly considering the nineteenth-century rise of patriotic armies. Emancipation emerged as a consensus in the Army, which became a relevant player in national politics after the war. The disproportional struggle to defeat a small contender such as Paraguay indicated that Brazil could not rely on slaves to defend its borders (Doratioto 2002, 484). Inspired by positivist ideals, most low-rank officials opposed not only slavery but also the parliamentary monarchy. Republicans and emancipationist quickly gained grounds in the Army (Carvalho 2003).

The emancipation movement was also popular among civilians. The growing urban population promoted anti-slavery demonstrations, and the cause found supporters in the press. Dom Pedro II was not against it, but slave labour was still the base of plantations in Rio de Janeiro and the Northeast, whose elites composed the backbone of the monarchy. Most noblemen were from those regions (Queiroz 1982). The conservative Prime Minister Rio Branco presented the "free womb law" in 1871, which freed new-born slaves and started a slow process of emancipation. The law did not count with full support among liberal congressmen, although the Liberal Party had traditionally attracted emancipationists (Carvalho 1988, 66). The following liberal cabinet failed to pass anti-slavery laws, and from then on most abolitionists became inclined to support the establishment of a republic (Carvalho 2003, 76).

The development of the coffee economy in São Paulo also challenged the monarchic status quo. Economic growth empowered the oligarchy of that state vis-à-vis the traditional elites from Rio de Janeiro and the Northeast. Besides coffee growers, merchants also grew rich in Santos and the capital São Paulo. The provincial government subsidised immigration from Europe, and the population increased much faster than the national average (Costa 1998, 728–29). In 1873, the *Paulistas* formed the Republican Party of São Paulo (PRP), the first well-structured republican institution in Brazil (Love 1994, 228). Already influential within the Army and the urban middle class, the emaciation cause gained support in the countryside of São Paulo in the 1880s as that state's farms swapped slave for immigrant labour (Fragoso 2000).

The Crown finally abolished slavery in 1888. Yet it failed to capitalise on that measure because most abolitionists were also republicans. Emancipation antagonised the traditional oligarchies, leaving the monarchy with rather slim support (Carvalho 1988, 76–77). The elderly and ill Dom Pedro II was politically isolated when Marshal Deodoro da Fonseca launched the quick and peaceful coup that deposed the monarchy and established the Republic in November 1889.

The Falling Empire and Its Exposed Bank

Seen from abroad, the Brazilian Empire was a solid state. Brazil arbitrated conflicts between Chile and Peru, and among the USA, France and Mexico in the 1880s (Rodrigues and Seitenfus 1995). Decades of political stability under a monarchic regime headed by an emperor connected to European royal families provided the Empire with international status (Topik 2014).

Macroeconomic fundamentals were also strong. External accounts were so favourable that the *mil-réis* reached its parity of 27 pence in the late 1880s, fully reverting the strong depreciation that took place during the Paraguayan War. The rising price and export volumes of coffee were the main drivers of the exchange rate appreciation, although foreign borrowing also played a role. The government issued many loans in London, increasing the stock of sovereign debt from £12.7 million in 1870 to £30.4 million in 1889 (Bouças 1955, 175). Most of this debt financed public works, but a significant share converted the domestic debt issued during the war into gold-denominated bonds. The domestic obligations paid a higher yield, but the operation increased the government's exposure to exchange rate fluctuation (Maria 1995, 120). This currency mismatch was not a problem in the 1880s, but it was going to cause a debt crisis of the following decade.

It was in under these benign conditions that the government contracted the largest and cheapest loan of the Empire in 1889. The loan was for £18.9 million, and the interest rate was 4%. The operation converted most of the country's old debt floated in London, which paid from 4.5% to 5% interests (Bouças 1955, 172–74). Meanwhile, a syndicate composed by Paribas and Barings attempted to break Rothschilds' monopoly by offering a £5 million credit line. Once Dom Pedro II fell, however, the syndicate withdrew the deal, claiming that its members did "not desire to open any credit to the newly established republican government."[10] That decision was expressed one month after the fall of the monarchy and about one year before the Baring Crisis. If the banks refused to lend to the newly established Brazilian Republic before the world financial meltdown of the early 1890s, they would certainly not have offered credit afterwards.

Only Rothschilds would underwrite Brazilian bonds after the collapse of the Empire. The bankers themselves declared, in a letter sent to the Brazilian government less than one month after the founding of the Republic, that "many persons (…) predict (…) a possible disintegration and dismemberment of your great country might take place."[11] Had Brazil been broken into several small nation states, the new governments would have likely defaulted on the monarchy's obligations. That was a great threat for Rothschilds, whose exposure to Brazil had grown together with the country's stock of sovereign debt.

Table 3.1 shows that Rothschilds participated in the issuing of over £1 billion in sovereign bonds between the 1850s and 1890s. Brazilian bonds made up to 8% of the total, behind France, the USA and Russia, but above Austria and Britain, two of the house's most traditional clients. This share is much larger when compared to the bonds the London House underwrote without partnerships: 31% of the total. While the bank issued Russian, French and US debt in association with other houses such as Barings and the Paris Rothschilds, Brazil's debt was an exclusive enterprise. The table also shows that Brazil was the only Latin American client until the bank established relations with Chile.

A Brazilian default would have ruined Rothschilds' reputation as an underwriter. No other client but Russia could have potentially harmed

[10] *AHP* Sauller (agent in London) to the Brazilian Government, 10 December 1889, 11/DFOM-333/14.

[11] *AR* Rothschilds to Ruy Barbosa (Finance Minister), 4 December 1889, XI/142/1886–1894.

Table 3.1 Breakdown of sovereign bonds underwritten by the London Rothschilds (*Source* Compiled from Ayers 1905)

	Brazil	*Austria*	*Britain*	*Chile*	*Egypt*	*France*	*Russia*	*USA*	*Others*	*Total*
	£ million									
London Rothschilds in association with other banks										
1810s–1850s	4.4	9.5	30.3			50.0				94.2
1860s	10.8	1.0					27.0		3.0	41.8
1870s	8.8	23.0	3.5		8.5	239.0	57.0	267.5	6.3	613.7
1880s	37.5	47.1		7.2	42.1		88.7			222.5
Total	61.5	80.6	33.8	7.2	50.6	289.0	172.7	267.5	9.3	972.2
Share (%)	6.3	8.3	3.5	0.7	5.2	29.7	17.8	27.5	1.0	100.0
London Rothschilds alone										
1810s–1850s	4.4	6.0	24.5							34.9
1860s	10.8								3.0	13.8
1870s	8.8		3.5						4.0	16.3
1880s	37.5			7.2	10.4		85.7			140.8
Total	61.5	6.0	28.0	7.2	10.4		85.7		7.0	205.8
Share (%)	29.9	2.9	13.6	3.5	5.1		41.6		3.4	100.0

Note "Austria" is both Austria and Hungary until 1867 and the Austro-Hungarian Empire after that date. "Others" include Italy, New Zealand, South Africa and Spain

the bank's default-free status as much as Brazil. Exposure was primarily reputational, but it also had financial consequences. The bank held a significant amount of Brazilian securities that summed up £1.26 million in 1889, most of which were government bonds. That was 5.25% of the house's total assets, enough to cause a loss but not to ruin its books.[12] Yet the bank's ability to profit from the underwriting of bonds depended on its status. Hence, a Brazilian default would have been financially detrimental in the long run. The bank would (and did) not let the new Republic on its own, as will become clear in Chapter 4.

Conclusion

Rothschilds' exposure and Brazil's reputation changed the balance of power between the bank and the government in favour of the latter. The bank was significantly strong vis-à-vis the government in the 1850s,

[12] *RA* I 000/77/4.

when both parts agreed on exclusivity. Rothschilds was not greatly exposed to Brazil, which had no solid reputation. By the time the monarchy fell, however, Brazil was a well-established borrower that ran sound policy in a peaceful country. Other underwriters were willing to contest Rothschilds' profitable monopoly. The issuing of many loans had increased the bank's exposure. Rothschilds had no choice but to remain associated with Brazil after the fall of the monarchy, which its managers correctly understood as a potentially dangerous event. The next chapter shows that the debt crisis of the 1890s increased the power of the government over the bank even further.

References

Archival Sources

AHP Archive Historique Paribas, Paris.
Brésil, Emprunt D´etat or.
RA Rothschild Archive, London.
Ledger Balance, I.
Correspondence, XI.

Official and Contemporary Sources

Ayers, Jules. 1905. *A Century of Finance, 1804 to 1904: The London House of Rothschild*. London: Neely.

Bouças, Valentim F. 1955. *Finanças do Brasil: dívida externa—1824–1945*. Rio de Janeiro: Ministério da Fazenda.

IBGE. 1990. *Estatísticas históricas do Brasil: séries econômicas, demográficas e sociais de 1550 a 1988*. Rio de Janeiro: Instituto Brasileiro de Geografia e Estatística.

Secondary Sources

Alencastro, Luiz Felipe. 2000. *O trato dos viventes: formação do Brasil no Atlântico Sul, séculos XVI e XVII*. São Paulo: Companhia das Letras.

Basile, Marcelo O. 2000. "O Império Brasileiro: panorama político." In *História geral do Brasil*, 188–245. Rio de Janeiro: Elsevier.

Bethell, Leslie. 1985. *Brazil: Empire and Republic, 1822–1930*. Cambridge: Cambridge University Press.

Cardoso, Ciro F. S., and Maria Y. Linhares. 2000. "A crise do colonialismo luso na América Portuguesa." In *História geral do Brasil*, 111–28. Rio de Janeiro: Campus.

Carneiro, David. 1983. *História da Guerra Cisplatina*. Brasília: Editora Universidade de Brasília.

Carvalho, José M. 1988. *Teatro de sombras: a política imperial*. Rio de Janeiro: IUPERJ.

———. 2003. *A construção da ordem: a elite imperial*. São Paulo: Editora Record.

Costa, Emília V. 1998. *Da monarquia à república: momentos decisivos*. São Paulo: UNESP.

Dawson, Frank G. 1990. *The First Latin American Debt Crisis: The City of London and the 1822–25 Loan Bubble*. New Haven: Yale University Press.

Doratioto, Francisco. 2002. *Maldita guerra: nova história da Guerra do Paraguai*. São Paulo: Companhia das Letras.

Flandreau, Marc, and Juan H. Flores. 2009. "Bonds and Brands: Foundations of Sovereign Debt Markets, 1820–1830." *The Journal of Economic History* 69 (3):646–84.

Fragoso, João L. 2000. "O império escravista e a república dos plantadores." In *História geral do Brasil*, 144–87. Rio de Janeiro: Campus.

Graham, Richard. 1977. "Government Expenditures and Political Change in Brazil, 1880–1899: Who Got What." *Journal of Interamerican Studies and World Affairs* 19 (3):339–68.

Jeffrey, D. Needell. 2006. *The Party of Order: The Conservatives, the State, And Slavery in the Brazilian Monarchy, 1831–1871*. Stanford: Stanford University Press.

Love, Joseph L. 1994. "Autonomia e interdependência: São Paulo e a Federação Brasileira, 1889–1937." In *História do Brasil*, edited by Boris Fausto, 58–83. São Paulo: EdUSP.

Lynch, John. 2001. *Argentine Caudillo: Juan Manuel de Rosas*. Lanham: Rowman & Littlefield Publishers.

Maria, B. Levy. 1995. "The Brazilian Public Debt—Domestic and Foreign, 1824–1913." In *La deuda pública en América Latina En Perspectiva Histórica*, edited by Reinhard Liehr, 212–30. Madrid: Iberoamericana.

Marichal, Carlos. 1989. *A Century of Debt Crises in Latin America: From Independence to the Great Depression, 1820–1930*. Princeton: Princeton University Press.

Mettenheim, Kurt. 2015. *Monetary Statecraft in Brazil: 1808–2014*. London: Routledge.

Minguzzi, Rubens B. 1974. *Código comercial brasileiro: Lei no. 556, de 25 de junho de 1850, incluindo legislação complementar, mercado de capitais, instituições financeiras, normas bancárias e outras*. São Paulo: J. Konfino.

Monteiro, Hamilton M. 2000. "Da Independência à vitória da ordem." In *História Geral Do Brasil*, 129–43. Rio de Janeiro: Elsevier.

Peláez, Carlos M., and Wilson Suzigan. 1981. *História monetária do Brasil.* Brasília: Editora Universidade de Brasília.

Queiroz, Suley R. 1982. *A abolição da escravidão.* Brasília: Editora Brasiliense.

Rodrigues, José H., and Ricardo A. S. Seitenfus. 1995. *Uma história diplomática do Brasil, 1531–1945.* Rio de Janeiro: Editora Record.

Shaw, Caroline S. 2005. "Rothschilds and Brazil: An Introduction to Sources in the Rothschild Archive." *Latin American Research Review* 40 (1):165–85.

Summerhill, William R. 2015. *Inglorious Revolution: Political Institutions, Sovereign Debt, and Financial Underdevelopment in Imperial Brazil.* New Haven: Yale University Press.

Summerhill, William R. 2018. "When is Debt Odious? Brazil and the Portuguese Loan of 1823." Manuscript.

Taylor, Alan M. 2003. "Foreign Capital in Latin America in the Nineteenth and Twentieth Centuries." Working Paper 9580. National Bureau of Economic Research.

Topik, Steven C. 2014. *The Political Economy of the Brazilian State, 1889–1930.* Austin: University of Texas Press.

Villela, André. 2001. "The Quest for Gold: Monetary Debates in Nineteenth-Century Brazil." *Revista de Economia Política* 21 (4):79–92.

Weller, Leonardo. 2015. "Rothschilds' 'Delicate and Difficult Task': Reputation, Political Instability, and the Brazilian Rescue Loans of the 1890s." *Enterprise & Society* 16 (2):381–412.

CHAPTER 4

Rothschilds' Troubled Republic: Brazil, 1889–1898

The Brazilian Empire was a well-established borrower when a republican coup deposed the monarchy in 1889. Reputation waned in the following decade. Political conflicts, some of which escalated into civil wars, forced the new republican administrations to overspend. Brazil did not default on its debt because Rothschilds underwrote rescue loans. This chapter analyses why the bank offered a credit umbrella to the government, and how high officials conditioned that outcome.

Brazil was Rothschilds' most exclusive client; hence a default would have ruined the bank's premier status. The Brazilian officials understood that the bank was exposed and acted accordingly. They pressured for rescue loans with which they could defend the new regime without damaging the country's clean debt record. The government free rode on the bank, which explains why it did not default nor did it consolidate fiscal accounts until the end of the decade. Lose economic policies were necessary for the consolidation of the Republic, even though they deteriorated payment capacity. Given the political turmoil of the 1890s and Rothschilds' credit umbrella, however, poor fiscal accounts were a relatively minor problem. Free riding explains why the crisis was so long: It started shortly after the first president took office, in 1889, and ended as a consequence of the 1898 Funding Loan.

The Funding Loan financed the payment of interests on the outstanding debt, and thus sharply reduced the debt burden. Rothschilds would only underwrite the funding bonds as long as the government raised taxation and reduced the monetary stock at a predetermined rate.

L. Weller, *Sovereign Debt Crises and Negotiations in Brazil and Mexico, 1888-1914*, https://doi.org/10.1007/978-3-319-73633-4_4

Economic activity collapsed and a severe crisis hit the coffee-growing state of São Paulo, but the deal appreciated the exchange rate, improved payment capacity and lowered Brazilian risk. The government borrowed at good conditions already in the early 1900s.

The literature stresses the power of Rothschilds over Brazil and presents the Funding Loan as an evidence of such domination.[1] I show in this chapter that the loan was a case of shared policy ownership rather than the unilateral imposition of orthodox policies. The Brazilians proposed the deal and threatened to default so that Rothschilds would accept it. Politics had stabilised by 1898, which permitted the finance minister to consolidate fiscal accounts without jeopardising the regime. The conditions on fiscal and monetary policies were instrumental for the government to appreciate the *mil-réis* in spite of the opposition of the coffee lobby. Rothschilds was a power broker that empowered policymakers committed to orthodox economic policies, in line with their peacetime priorities.

Regime Change, Chaos and Stabilisation

Contemporaries did not anticipate the fall of the Brazilian monarchy, either domestically or abroad. Rothschilds was still in the process of underwriting the Empire's best loan ever when a military coup deposed Dom Pedro II. The imperial state had been under pressure from emergent social groups—the Army, the oligarchy of São Paulo and the urban middle classes (Graham 1977, 340, 341). The emperor had prevented conflicts from disrupting the status quo, so the absence of such a unifying figure destabilised politics as opposing groups ascended nationally.

The core motivation of the coup was a personal dispute involving Marshal Deodoro da Fonseca (1889–1891) and members of the monarchy's last cabinet. Fonseca did not intend to change the regime, but the Crown fell together with its last administration (Costa 1998, 456). Fonseca was appointed president and started what became known as the Sword Republic, a five-year period during which militaries controlled the Executive Branch. His presidency preceded the administration of Floriano Peixoto (1891–1894), who was also a marshal. Nevertheless, the Army divided the political arena state with São Paulo's PRP, the party that controlled the first republican assembly in Congress.

[1] See Flandreau and Flores (2010, 18) for a recent contribution.

President Peixoto and the *Paulistas* diverged on the relative power of the central government: The former was in favour of a strong presidency; the latter defended the transfer of power to local authorities. Congress approved a Constitution in 1891 that relocated the collection of export duties from the central to the state governments. The new tax code disproportionably favoured coffee-growing São Paulo, which responded to a large share of the country's exports. Fonseca closed the house in the first of the many coups of Brazil's republican history. The government also censored the press, which had been free during the Second Reign. The liberal state of the monarchic regime quickly eroded as the institutions that had conciliated liberals and conservatives for decades vanished with those two parties (Carvalho 1988, 182).

Besides the *Paulistas*, Fonseca needed to deal with Navy officers who feared that he would re-establish the monarchy. The rebels mobilised gunboats in Rio de Janeiro's Guanabara Bay and forced the president to resign in 1891 (Love 1994, 249). Vice-President Peixoto reopened Congress but ruled by decree. The "iron marshal," as Peixoto was known, delayed the establishment of the federalist system arranged by the 1891 Constitution, which accentuated the political polarisation between those against and in favour of decentralisation (Topik 2014, 267).

The dispute became violent in the southern state of Rio Grande do Sul, whose long history of wars and separatism dates back to colonial times. Peixoto supported Governor Júlio de Castilhos, a local dictator who imposed an authoritarian regime in that state. Castilhos repressed an opposition group that included landowners with close links with neighbouring Uruguay and Argentina. A rebel Army took the state capital Porto Alegre and marched north, nearly reaching São Paulo. The Federalist Revolution threatened the republican state and the integrity of the national territory. Meanwhile, the Navy revolted for the second time in less than three years, this time in support of the Federalist Revolution. The conflict was so intense that European and US gunboats intervened to safeguard trading ships under their respective flags (Topik 2000, 238–45).

Topik (2014, 225) describes the politics in the first years of the Republic as "chaotic." Carvalho (2003, 184–91) concludes that "the survival of the new regime was in serious danger." Stakes were so high that the PRP reached a compromise with President Peixoto. The *Paulistas* supported the campaign against the Federalist Revolution. In return, the president abstained from interfering in the upcoming election, scheduled for 1894, and in the implementation of the 1891 Constitution (Schulz 1994, 185–89). The Army suppressed the Navy revolt with the help of the Americans and pushed the Federalist Revolutionaries back to Rio Grande do Sul.[2]

Prudente de Morais (1894–1898), the candidate of the PRP and head of Congress during the 1891 Constitution, was elected Brazil's first civil president. Morais negotiated the end of the Federalist Revolution in mid-1895 but was the target of low-ranking officers and unorganised crowds in the streets of Rio de Janeiro (Fausto 2007, 47; Schulz 1994, 198). Known as Jacobinos after the radicals of the French Revolution, the rioters believed that the Republic needed an authoritarian marshal such as Peixoto instead of an aristocrat civilian such as Morais (Queiroz 1986). The death of Peixoto in 1896 fuelled the Jacobinos' movement (Topik 2000, 184–91).

Riots intensified as the government failed to win the Canudos War, the second large-scale conflict of the 1890s. Local and federal troops fought the followers of a religious leader who claimed for the return of the monarchy. The group settled in Canudos, in the impoverished hinterland of Bahia, and defeated one military expedition after the other. The war galvanised the Jacobinos, to whom only the return of the Sward Republic would restore order across the country. The turmoil reached a climax in 1897 when tens of thousands of troops finally won the Canudos War, leaving almost no survivals among the twenty thousand men, women and children who lived in the area (Moniz 1987). The government subsequently suppressed the rioters in Rio de Janeiro, following an attempt to assassinate the president (Queiroz 1986, 75–80). Morais survived his term in office and peacefully handed over the presidency to his fellow PRP member Manuel de Campos Sales (1898–1902). That marked the pacification of Brazil and the beginning of a three-decade-long era during which the PRP governed the country in association with other regional parties. In the following years, isolated conflicts did not threaten the stability of the oligarchic republican regime (Fausto 2007, 53).

[2]The USA was one of the first countries to accept the republican state. Its interference in that conflict was part of its debut as a world power, active in the geopolitics of the Western Hemisphere. Topik (2000, 274) speculates that the USA pressured for the agreement between the *Paulistas* and President Peixoto.

The Fiscal Collapse

The 1890s were also turbulent in respect of economic policy. The last monarchic cabinet created a system of emission banks designed to provide credit for the farmers hit by the 1888 abolition of slavery (Schulz 1996, 68–70). Ruy Barbosa, the first finance minister of the Republic, used this new financial infrastructure to increase the monetary stock in an attempt to promote economic growth. Barbosa was a well-known intellectual influenced by the nineteenth-century monetary quantitative theory. The minister afirmed that Brazil's sparse population and backward transportation system kept the velocity of circulation of money at low levels. The government needed to print money to promote economic growth in spite of those structural problems. He also claimed that the emancipation of slaves and immigration boosted the labour market, increasing the demand for money. Hence, an expansionist monetary policy would not result in high inflation (Barbosa 1892). The new government not only enforced the issuing rights of the institutions created in 1888 but also established joint stock banks. Barbosa intended to develop the domestic financial sector so that it would transfer savings from the coffee into the commercial and the incipient industrial sectors (Peláez and Suzigan 1981, 150, 178–79).

Instead of building the dynamic financial system the country needed, Barbosa's policies resulted in a financial bubble. A profusion of new companies appeared in the Rio Stock Exchange, and the rise in credit quickly lifted their share prices. The bubble burst in 1891 in an episode known as *encilhamento*—the Portuguese word for the minutes that precede horse races. The new monetary policy was excessively loose and M_2 increased by 144.9% between 1890 and 1891, against an annual average of 0.7% in the 1880s (IBGE 1990, 535–37). Brazil's financial sector was too backward for such a monetary expansion.[3] Monetary printing depreciated the *mil-réis* by 40% between 1889 and 1891, as shown in Table 4.1. Annual inflation in Rio de Janeiro reached 25% in 1891 against an average of 1% in the 1880s (Catão 1992). Falling real wages fuelled the riots that shook the capital in the 1890s (Meade 1989, 224). Barbosa left office in 1891 under severe criticism, and during the rest of the decade a succession of finance ministers tried to deal with the consequences of the *encilhamento*.

[3]Summerhill (2015) argues that the government maintained the financial sector backward during the Empire.

Table 4.1 Brazil's financial data (*Source* IBGE (1990, 312, 541–42, 591–93) for monetary growth, coffee price and exchange rate; Balanço da receita e despeza da república and IBGE (1990, 617–18) for primary surplus; Bouças (1955, 220) for sovereign debt services)

	Monetary growth (M_2, %)	*Coffee price (£/bag)*	*Exchange rate (pense/ mil-réis)*	*Primary surplus (£ million)*	*Sovereign debt service (£ million)*	*SD service (% tax revenue)*
1889	0.3	3.49	27.20	2.06	1.67	9.2
1890	59.5	3.27	22.64	2.11	1.66	9.0
1891	85.4	3.10	16.35	4.30	1.64	10.5
1892	−2.8	4.09	11.94	0.33	1.62	14.3
1893	−9.9	3.74	11.56	0.91	1.78	14.3
1894	12.5	3.33	10.09	−1.89	1.76	15.8
1895	0.0	2.92	9.90	1.68	2.11	16.6
1896	1.5	1.74	9.02	2.22	2.08	16.0
1897	6.6	1.49	7.73	0.45	2.04	20.9
1898	4.8	1.48	7.20	−7.34	2.09	21.5

The exchange rate depreciation raised the fiscal burden of servicing the sovereign debt. To make matters worse, the devolution of taxation on exports to the states arranged under the 1891 Constitution shrunk the central government's tax base. The ratio between the services due on the sovereign debt and tax revenue increased by over one-third in 1892, when the new tax code was under effect. That was the first time since the Paraguayan War that the government did not run enough primary surplus to honour the sovereign debt.[4]

Coffee prices assumed a persistent downward cycle in the mid-1890s. European migrants found work in new coffee groves in São Paulo. The local government used a share of the taxes it now collected from exports to subsidise immigration and the construction of a state railway network.

[4]Ferguson (1998, 346) measures payment capacity by comparing the required services on the sovereign debt with expenditure. According to his calculations, that ratio remained relatively low, at 10.5% between 1890 and 1899, from which he concludes that the debt crisis was mild. Ferguson's interpretation is misleading because expenditure was much higher than tax revenue due to warfare, one of the leading causes of the crisis. I evaluate payment capacity based on the ratio between services and tax revenue, which shows a more realistic picture of the government's capacity to meet debt services. Such ratio is common in the literature; see, for instance, Flandreau and Zumer (2004, 31).

Coffee production soared and São Paulo started to produce about half of the world's output (Bacha and Greenhill 1992, 305–7). On the demand side, the habit of drinking coffee was already widespread in the USA, the largest consumer market. The demand was significant inelastic regarding both prices and income, which means that it would not match the rise in supply. Coffee responded to over 60% of Brazil's exports. Hence the fall in prices reduced the trade surplus and contributed to the depreciation of the *mil-réis* (IBGE 1990, 569, 616).

Nonetheless, politics was more important than foreign trade as the main driver of the debt crisis. The price of coffee was high when payment capacity started to deteriorate and low when it improved, respectively at the beginning and the end of the 1890s.[5] Politics prevented the government from appreciating the exchange rate in the aftermath of the *encilhamento*. The Peixoto administration attempted to implement a tight monetary policy to strengthen the *mil-réis* and control inflation, but the fiscal deficit limited the extent to which it could withdraw money from circulation. The decentralisation of taxation reduced revenue, while the Federalist Revolution expanded the military budget (Triner 2000, 46; Schulz 1996, 111–15). As a result, the government resumed printing money in 1994, a policy that continued under President Morais, this time to finance the Canudos War. But now coffee prices were falling, which put extra pressure on the *mil-réis*.

The government would only be able to appreciate the *mil-réis* once it could devote a substantial amount of tax revenue to tighten the monetary base rather than to sustain an expensive military budget.[6] The solvency problem was not permanent because the country had the means to generate enough wealth for the government to pay its obligations—it ran a fiscal surplus in the 1900s (IBGE 1990, 535–36, 617–18). The question of how long Brazil would remain insolvent depended on when the political situation would finally stabilise.

[5] This point appears in Peláez and Suzigan (1981, 167), Franco (1983) and Schulz (1996, 118–19).

[6] Franco (2014, 25–26) and Schulz (1996, 101–13) also acknowledge that political instability led to fiscal deterioration and exchange rate depreciation. Flandreau and Zumer (2004, 34, 53) put Brazil in perspective when they characterise it as a troubled borrower during the 1890s because of both the currency mismatch problem and the country's unsound tax prospects.

The contemporary press understood the extent of the debt crisis. In 1895, *The Economist* noted that "if strenuous and successful efforts [are] not made to economize in every direction, Brazil will follow some of its neighbours into the ranks of the insolvent."[7] The crisis continued, and in 1898 that same newspaper concluded that a "default in the service of the foreign debt is regarded locally as only a matter of time."[8] Similarly, *The Investor's Monthly Manual* expected a "*fin-de-siècle* expedient of a moratorium," and *The Investor's Review* reported that "the rate of exchange barometer [...] points straight to national insolvency."[9] However, the government did not "economize in every direction," as *The Economist* had advised, nor did it implement the "expedient of a moratorium." It did not have to do so because of Rothschilds' credit umbrella.

Rothschilds' Credit Umbrella

The market reacted to the crisis and Brazilian risk increased from 1.7% in October 1889 (one month before the fall of the monarchy) to a peak of 7.5% in July 1898. Risk started to rise right after the fall the republican coup and the ascent accelerated between 1891 and 1892 as the Navy revolted and the *mil-réis* depreciated. Brazilian risk recovered slightly when Peixoto administration restored order in Rio de Janeiro and implemented a short-lived tight monetary policy, but rose once more during the Federalist Revolution and the Canudos War.[10]

The Baring Crisis of 1890 probably played a role in the rise of Brazilian risk.[11] Yet politics were so unstable and fiscal results were so poor in Brazil that domestic conditions alone are enough to explain the spike in borrowing costs. The average sovereign risk applied to borrowing countries excluding Brazil (Russia, Ottoman Empire, Argentina, Portugal, Greece, Mexico, Uruguay, Chile, Sweden, China, Hungary and Japan) fell from a peak of 2.96% in 1893

[7] *The Economist*, 27 July 1895, issue 2711, p. 14.

[8] *The Economist*, 23 April 1898, issue 2852, p. 8.

[9] *The Investor's Review*, 29 April 1898, vol. 18, p. 599; *The Investor's Monthly Manual*, 31 May 1898, vol. 28, p. 225.

[10] See Fig. 1.1.

[11] Fishlow (1995) suggests that the external crisis was not determinant, but Mitchener and Weidenmier (2008) found evidence of contagion.

to a low of 1.97% in 1899.[12] The coefficient of variation between this emergent index and Brazilian risk was negative (−0.24) during that period. Brazil lost credibility as the world recovered from the Baring Crisis.

Rothschilds underwrote loans and short-term treasury notes for £13.1 million between 1893 and 1895.[13] Although the 1893 loan officially funded the building of the Western of Minas Railways, 63% of the net revenue financed the campaign against the Federalist Revolution. The government contracted more credit to pay for the conflict in early 1895 when it issued £2 million in treasury notes with maturities from nine to fifteen months.[14] Later that year, Rothschilds underwrote a second large loan to redeem the treasuries and to cover services on the sovereign debt.

The 1893 and 1895 loans carried a 5% interest rate and were issued at 80% and 85% discounts, respectively. The risk premiums—3.75% and 3.53%—were considerably higher than the average risk applied to the monarchic loans—2.23%.[15] However, the 1893 loan was cheap relative to the credit Brazil had on the secondary market: It was issued at 90% of Brazilian risk.[16] Rothschilds was providing credit at a rate the government would not be able to find on the market, which qualifies that operation as a rescue loan. The 1895 loan was not as generous, but it was not far above Brazilian risk, and its revenue was providential for Brazil to pay for the short-term obligations issued during the Federalist Revolution.

As the government borrowed, Rothschilds became more exposed to Brazil. Table 4.2 shows the breakdown of the Rothschilds-branded bonds floating on the London Stock Exchange in July 1893 and 1898, just before the issuing of those years' Brazilian loans. The contracts of the 1893 and 1895 loans did not require yearly amortisations, which was

[12]These countries are the ones used in a similar index by Mauro et al. (2006, 30). Calculated from *The Investor's Monthly Manual.*

[13]This amount corresponds to 36% of the tax collected in the period and 44% of what the state owed to foreign bondholders up to then. Calculated from IBGE (1990, 616), and Bouças (1955, 192).

[14]*RA* Finance Minister Rodrigues Alves to Rothschilds, 31 December 1894, XI/142/401F/6.

[15]Average weighted according to the amount issued in each loan. From Bouças (1955, 113–73) and *The Investor's Monthly Manual.*

[16]From IBGE (1990), *BHMF* 332/225 and *The Investor's Monthly Manual.*

Table 4.2 Breakdown of sovereign bonds underwritten by Rothschilds and floating on the market, 1893 and 1898 (*Source* Calculated from *The Investor's Monthly Manual*)

	July 1893		*July 1898*	
	£ million	*% of total*	*£ million*	*% of total*
Brazil	32.59	22	47.72	27
Russia	91.33	62	95.46	55
Chile	9.00	6	15.55	9
Britain	9.00	6	11.98	7
Others	5.30	4	4.19	2

Note "Others" are Austro-Hungary, Egypt, Italy, Ottoman Empire and Spain

current practice at the time (Bouças 1955, 191–94). The bank avoided imposing an extra burden on its client. Brazil was thus borrowing without retiring the new debt, which explains why its share had the greatest increase among Rothschilds' clients, from 22% to 27%. Although still the second larger borrower in size, it was quickly approaching the first one: The ratio between the Brazilian and Russia shares raised from one-third in 1894 to half in 1898.

While Rothschilds was becoming more exposed to Brazil in terms of reputation, it was also reducing its financial exposure. Figure 4.1 reports the bank's portfolio of Brazilian sovereign bonds calculated at par, unaffected by depreciation. The house also held stocks of Brazilian companies, but that corresponded to only 11% its Brazilian portfolio. I did not include company stocks because Rothschilds' balance sheets reported only its market value. The portfolio fell in the early 1890s, which means that the bank sold Brazilian bonds during the crisis that hit the country after the regime change.

Nevertheless, the bank did not manage to decrease the Brazilian portfolio to less than 3% of its total assets during the 1890s. The steep fall in the Brazilian portfolio lost momentum in the mid-1890s, during the worst of the crisis. That happened because Rothschilds held 9% of the 1893 loan, 23% of the 1895 treasury notes and 12% of the 1895 loan.[17] The bank was playing roles of both underwriter and bondholder,

[17] *RA* I/158/000/77/4.

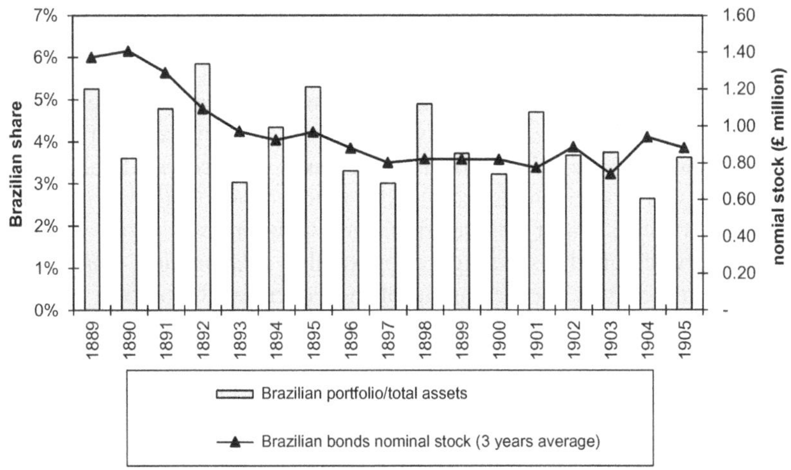

Fig. 4.1 Brazilian sovereign debt portfolio held by Rothschilds, 1889–1905 (*Source* Calculated from *RA* I/158/000/77/4)

similarly to what it had done in 1829 but in contrast with its usual business.

In a cable to the Finance Minister (and future president) Rodrigues Alves (1894–1896), one of the bank's managers informed that "our friends" took the bulk of the debt.[18] Rothschilds was working with its closest associates in London to "support the markets to a large extent, to prevent a really serious fall in the price."[19] Yet the price of the country's debt collapsed in the following years. The quotation of the 1893 and 1895 bonds reached 44% and 49% of par in the first half of 1898, way below their respective issuing discount of 80% and 85%.[20] The debt crisis continued in spite of Rothschilds' credit umbrella because of Brazil's loose economic policy.

[18] *RA* Rothschilds to Rodrigues Alves, 26 July 1895, XI/142/1895–1900.

[19] Ibid.

[20] *The Investor's Monthly Manual*, January to June 1898, vol. 28, pp. 1–6.

Brazil as a Free Rider

Rothschilds' credit umbrella reduced the probability of a default, thereby raising the incentives for the Brazilian government to implement policies that reduced payment capacity: Increasing military expenditure and decentralising taxation. The government could have serviced the sovereign debt with its resources had it not launched one of the above policies, which means that it was free riding on Rothschilds.

The services on the sovereign debt totalled £9.8 million from 1893 to 1897, respectively the beginning of the Federalist Revolution and the end of the Canudos War. It makes sense to exclude the 1893 and 1895 loans from this counterfactual, as they financed wars and debt services. Without this lending, the figure falls to £7.8 million, the equivalent of 13.3% of tax revenue.[21] Combined, the budgets of the Army and the Navy accounted for an average of 23.1% of tax revenue from 1890 to 1892, which then increased to 36.5% in the following five years. Thus, war expenditure consumed an extra 13.4% of taxation.[22] Hence the government would have had funds to honour its foreign financial obligations without further loans had the military budget remained constant.

Similarly, had the central government continued taxing exports as it did before 1893, it would also have had sufficient resources to service the sovereign debt. Between 1890 and 1892, the government taxed on average 4.9% of exports, while from 1893 to 1897 the exports were worth £149.3 million. Applying that rate to the later period suggests that, had the government not regionalised that duty, it would have received an extra £7.2 million in export duties, which corresponds to 13.8% of annual tax revenue—this was also sufficient to service the sovereign debt.[23] This proportion is even higher with alternative base years. Taxation on exports

[21] Calculate from Bouças (1955, 220) and IBGE (1990, 616–18).

[22] This comparison should not include the period before 1890 because the Army budget grew after the 1889 coup, mainly due to the increase in military salaries, which is natural given the character of the republican movement. See Caravalho (2005, 54–56) and Schulz (1994, 145). The rise in the defence budget appears greater if we include the earlier period. It is 14.3% if the base years are 1889–1892. Calculated from *Balanço da receita e despeza da República* for the military budget and IBGE (1990, 617–18) for federal expenditure.

[23] Calculated from *Balanço da receita e despesa da República* for tax revenue from exports and IBGE (1990, 535–36) for exports. This counterfactual is based on the assumption that eventual changes in export tariffs after the regionalisation of the duty did not affect exports significantly, which is consistent with the literature on the Brazilian coffee economy. The demand is inelastic, varying according to taste. Investment has a long maturity term, and in the short term, the supply is also inelastic. See Topik (1999), Furtado (2007) and Bacha and Greenhill (1993).

was already low in 1892, an early consequence of the 1891 Constitution. Taking 1890–1891 as base years, for instance, the share reaches to 20.4%. In strict fiscal terms, Brazil could have avoided the debt crisis of the 1890s.

Given the period's turmoil and the credit at hand, the government had strong incentives to go into extra debt; the alternative would have entailed politically prohibitive costs. The government needed to increase military expenditure because the Federalist Revolution threatened the integrity of the national territory, while the resistance of the rebels in Canudos intensified riots in Rio de Janeiro. According to Love (1994, 70), the regional oligarchies, above all São Paulo's PRP, supported the 1889 republican coup in the hope that the new regime would implement a less centralised tax system. The 1891 Constitution met those expectations. Blocking the transfer of taxation to the states would have antagonised the oligarchy of São Paulo and thus jeopardised the stability of the regime. Finally, unsound fiscal policy conditioned the issuing of paper money that depreciated the national currency. The weak *mil-réis* was another demand from the *Paulistas* for it protected the coffee sector from falling international prices (Topik 2014, 35–37; Triner 2000, 36–37).

Rothschilds understood the consequences of those unsound but politically crucial policies. In a cable sent before the issuing of the 1895 loan, the bankers wrote to Minister Rodrigues Alves that they had been "watch[ing] with great regret the further decline in the exchange [rate]," which they believed was the consequence of "the large additional issue of paper money during the [Federalist] revolution, and also the considerable deficit in the Budget." Following such a precise interpretation, the bankers attempted to make the lending conditional on new policies. They explained to Rodrigues Alves that there was a "possible chance [that] there might be, later in the present year [1895], a large External Loan," as long as a "substantial share" of the borrowing financed the implementation of a tight monetary policy. Rothschilds also suggested the introduction of new "import duties [that] would of course have to be raised in gold, and would have to be applied exclusively to finance the service of the External Debt and the withdrawal of paper money."[24]

The bankers did not introduce any mechanism to enforce the application of these measures, and Brazil ended up breaking the agreement. Rodrigues Alves promised that the loan would "meet extraordinary

[24] *RA* Rothschilds to Rodrigues Alves, 21 January 1895, XI/142/1895–1900. Emphasis in the original.

expenses of the revolt and provide redemption of paper money,"[25] but the government resumed printing it.[26] A few weeks after launching the 1895 loan, the minister informed Rothschilds that "it is not licit [for the government] to charge taxes of any sort in gold: Only the Congress has the prerogative [...] on the matter."[27] The government introduced a new tax on imports that was not pegged to gold, and the revenue fell vis-à-vis the obligations on the sovereign debt as the exchange rate depreciated.[28] Why did Rothschilds accept such loosely defined policy conditions? Political instability appears to be the answer. While the bank and the government were negotiating the lending, Rodrigues Alves explained that:

> Unfortunately the South is not yet appeased. The federalists have no elements to march and their action is restricted to the border, but they will continue [...] disturbing the action of the government, demanding large warfare sacrifices.[29]

In other words, the minister communicated that the government was about to pacify the country, even though the war demanded "large" human and financial resources. The message was accurate on the location and capability of the rebels, and therefore the prospect of victory, but it exaggerated the government's struggle in the fighting at that stage, which was not near the level of the previous years (Reverbel 1985, 89). Given the available information, however, it was rational for Rothschilds to continue supporting its client without enforcing conditions that would have reduced its ability to secure national order. The bankers were waiting for the end of warfare to pressure for fiscal consolidation. Brazil was not at peace until 1898, when Rothschilds underwrote a new loan. This time the bank conditioned the lending on well-enforced conditions.

[25] *RA* Rodrigues Alves do Rothschilds, 16 February 1895, XI/65/9.

[26] See Table 4.1.

[27] *RA* Rodrigues Alves to Rothschilds, 11 March 1895, XI/65/9B/1895–96.

[28] The customs on imports increased 120% between 1894 and 1898, but only 56% when measured in pounds. Calculated from *Balaço da Receita e Despesa da República*.

[29] *RA* Rodrigues Alves to Rothschilds, 11 March 1895, XI/65/9B.

The Funding Loan as Shared Policy Ownership

The debt crisis reached a climax in 1898. The conjunction of loose economic policies and falling coffee prices depreciated the *mil-réis* to record levels, and the services on the sovereign debt required the greatest proportion of tax revenue since the establishment of the republic.[30] Rothschilds rescued Brazil once more, but this time the bankers enforced conditions on economic policy that improved payment capacity in the following decade. However, the government still needed to threaten to default to make Rothschilds underwrite the loan.

In a conference with the bankers, Azevedo Castro, an agent of the Brazilian Treasury in London, mentioned the high risk of "payment suspension" and proposed an agreement that would include a "large loan" and allow a coordinated "suspension of services." Castro reported to the Finance Minister Bernardino de Campos (1896–1898) that the bankers appeared to be "reticent" about the proposition and declared themselves "very concerned about the possibility of unilateral action by Brazil."[31] Minister Campos contacted Rothschilds directly a month later in March 1898. Rothschilds communicated that it would be "impossible to issue" new bonds because "the 5% 1895 loan issued at 85 is now only 65." Nevertheless, they considered a £5 million loan at 6% interest as long as the government leased the Central Railway, a state-owned line that connected Rio de Janeiro to São Paulo.[32] Rothschilds had presented this proposal to the government in the previous year, on behalf of the British company Greenwood, which, once in charge of the railway, intended to peg tariffs to gold.[33]

President Morais turned down the offer. Officially, Morais claimed that the leasing was illegal, but, in a letter to Minister Campos, he stated his goal to arrange a larger and cheaper lending facility without any conditions on railways. The president argued that:

[30] See Table 4.1.

[31] *BHMF* Azevedo Castro (Treasury) to Bernardino de Campos, 18 February 1898, 332/532.

[32] *RA* Rothschilds to Bernardino de Campos, 7 March 1898, XI/142/1895–1900.

[33] *RA* Rothschilds to Bernardino de Campos, 18 and 30 October and 26 November 1897, XI/65/10A.

> *£5 million would not provide the necessary support for the plan of restructuration of our finances (...) it is possible that the Jews would change their position once they are faced with the facts, if we insinuate that we will be fatally forced to suspend payments abroad if we do not obtain the loan.*[34]

The threat was genuine—the president admitted to Minister Campos that "if they insist on the impossibility of the loan it will be impossible to avoid the suspension of payments."[35] The government was supposed to pay £1.91 million in services on the sovereign debt by the end of 1898, although it ran a primary deficit of £1.05 million in 1897, which grew even more in the following year.[36] With the exchange rate at a historically low level, printing money and borrowing domestically was not an option to cover the foreign-denominated payments due on the sovereign debt.

The threat worked, and Rothschilds decided to "communicate with the Council of Foreign Bondholders" and to "use [its] best endeavor to induce them to accept the propositions contained in your message."[37] The "proposition" was the Funding Loan: The issuing of 5 percent-type bonds totalling £8.6 million to replace interest payments until 1901. In other words, the bondholders received the so-called funding bonds rather than cash in the following three years. Moreover, Brazil became free from amortising the debt until 1911.

The Funding Loan included a deal on economic policy that was similar to what both parties had loosely agreed in 1895. This time, the contract made the conditions explicit and included a self-enforcement mechanism. The government was supposed to burn paper money in an amount equivalent to the funding bonds the bank was going to float until 1901. Rothschilds also required the introduction of a new duty on imports collected in gold to finance the withdrawal of money from circulation. The Rio de Janeiro branch of the London and River Plate Bank—a British rather than a Brazilian bank, and thus freer from the government's influence—was in charge of verifying whether the government was burning paper money as agreed. Had the Brazilians failed to

[34] *IHGB* Prudente de Morais to Bernardino de Campos, 8 March 1898, ACP66/DL 572. Emphasis in the original.

[35] *IHGB* Prudente de Morais to Bernardino de Campos, 3 April 1898, ACP66/DL 592.

[36] Calculated from Balanço da Despesa e Receita da República.

[37] *RA* Rothschilds to Bernardino de Campos, 31 May 1898, XI/65/6.

implement the new policies, Rothschilds would have suspended the loan, forcing the borrower to resume interest payments in cash.[38]

The London bondholders and the British press received the Funding Loan coldly, but they did not repudiate the deal. Although the Corporation of Foreign Bondholders refused to endorse the operation, it did not officially characterise the scheme as a default.[39] Likewise, *The Economist* stated that "the bondholders have the clearest ground for protesting against [the operation because] they have neither been advised nor consulted." In the same full page report, however, the periodical recognised that the suspension of amortisation was an appropriate measure, given that "it would, of course, be absurd to attempt to keep up the sinking-fund purchase while the Government is practically claiming its inability to meets its current expenses."[40] *The Economist* explained that the conditions placed on monetary policy would "lift" the exchange rate, making it possible for the government to "accumulate on this side a gold fund, which would be available when the payment of interest in cash is resumed." All depended on the "engagement on the part of the Government not to make any fresh issue of paper money."[41] *The Times* mentioned this point more amicably, praising the agreement on monetary policy as "most important [...] as regards the future of Brazil."[42]

These passages suggest a reason why bondholders accepted the Funding Loan: There was a good chance that the appreciation of the exchange rate would raise the quotation of the Brazilian debt, thereby recovering the losses of the previous decade. Expectations were correct, for the prices of the 1893 and 1895 bonds surpassed the issuing discount in 1901 and reached 100% of face value in 1905. The funding bonds appreciated to higher levels. From the first quotation of 81% in October 1898, the price increased to a peak of 106% in June 1905.[43]

Rothschilds exercised its influence over the market, arranging a deal on behalf of the bondholders. In the end, the final creditors accepted the operation, and the house did not lose its default-free reputation. Rather than

[38] *BHMF* 332/225.

[39] Brazil was not blacklisted in the *Annual Report of the Corporation of Foreign Bondholders*.

[40] *The Economist*, 18 June 1898, issue 2860, p. 904.

[41] Ibid.

[42] *The Times*, 16 June 1898, issue 3554, p. 9.

[43] *The Investor's Monthly Manual*, June 1905, vols. 28, 31, 35.

a default, which happens when borrowers halt service payments unilaterally, the Funding Loan was a debt re-contracting arrangement. The bank also exercised its power over the government when it pressured for monetary tightening, but the agreement was a case of shared policy ownership rather than policy imposition. The Brazilians not only proposed the loan but also negotiated its conditions. Rothschilds at first intended to carry out the paper burning at 16 pence per *mil-réis*. At that level, the Funding Loan would have reduced the money supply (M_2) by 34%. Minister Campos argued that such a low rate would have caused "embarrassments to the National Treasury."[44] Rothschilds accepted the rate the government proposed, 18 pence, at which M_2 fell by 31%.[45] The agreement on monetary policy did reduce liquidity shaply, but the consequences would have been more extreme had the government not negotiated.

Rothschilds as a Power Broker

Brazilian officials were more inclined to implement tight economic policy in 1898 than in 1895. Political stabilisation switched the government's priorities, raising the payoffs of fiscal consolidation. A few months before the launching of the Funding Loan, Finance Minister (and future president) Campos Sales informed Rothschilds that exchange rate depreciation was a "bottomless pit without which Brazil would already have converted the 1890s fiscal deficits into surpluses."[46] Perhaps the minister went too far in his claim, but the exchange rate did deteriorate payment capacity. Had the foreign value of the *mil-réis* remained constant at the 1889 level, services would have increased mildly in 1895 and decreased afterwards. Had the Funding Loan not been arranged and the exchange rate remained at the level it was in 1898, services would have reached an all times record in 1901.[47]

[44] *BHMF* Bernardino de Campos to Rothschilds, June 1898, 332/532.

[45] Figures calculated from the ratios expressed in *BHMF* Bernardino de Campos to Rothschilds, June 1898, 332/532, and IBGE (1990, 542).

[46] *BHMF* Bernardino de Campos to Rothschilds, 25 January 1898, 332/532.

[47] Calculated from *Bouças* (1955) and IBGE (1990, 591–93, 616–18). These contrafactual trends should be considered with caution as they do not take inflation into consideration, but they are useful to demonstrate the impact of exchange rate depreciation in raising the cost of servicing the sovereign debt.

One could assume that Minister Campos Sales was simulating an intention to change economic policy, as his predecessor had done in 1895. Nevertheless, a few months later, already as a president-elected, Campos Sales (1898–1902) sent a cable to Bernardino de Campos, his successor in the Ministry of Finance, stating the need for "persistence and effort towards good financial management" to "reestablish" the Brazilian credit.[48] Campos Sales wrote from London, where he was negotiating the Funding Loan. Once in office, he appointed Joaquim Murtinho as the new finance minister. Murtinho was a senator who had built a political career by criticising the loose monetary policy of the 1890s. In 1897, he joined the Morais administration as the minister of industry, trade and railways (Peláez and Suzigan 1981, 182–83).[49] Given his orthodox credentials, Murtinho's political rise indicates that the government indeed intended to defend the value of the national currency.

Rothschilds probably learned a lesson from the 1895 loan and introduced well-enforced conditions on the Funding Loan to prevent the government from cheating again. Yet this is not the complete story. The change in approach to economic policy within the government reflected the country's pacification. It is not clear how much Rothschilds knew that the country had pacified by 1898. Yet the Brazilian crisis had become one of the bank's top priorities, and its managers followed that country's internal affairs closely. Their decision to enforce sound economic policy was consistent with the new political conditions. It worked as a tool through which high officials such as President Campos Sales and Minister Murtinho adjusted the priorities of the government after the end of the Canudos War. Once the turmoil was over, it became more important to "reestablish" the credit of the country (as President Campos Sales had put it) than to finance warfare—military expenditure (Army and Navy) fell from 18% to 10% of the total budget between 1898 and 1899 and only returned to the level of 1897 in 1910.[50]

[48] *BHMF* Campos Sales to Bernardino de Campos, 2 May 1898, 332/532. Abreu (2002, 520) recognises Campos Sales' commitment to sound policies when running for office.

[49] Paláez and Suzigan (1981, 182–83).

[50] *Balanço da Receita e Despesa da República*.

Rothschilds played the role of a power broker in favour of high officials committed to orthodox policies, who became politically stronger as the country pacified. This alliance between bank and policymakers balanced the power of groups that benefited from the weak *mil-réis*, namely the coffee exporters. The Funding Loan was surely instrumental: Without it, Murtinho would not have had the political capacity to tight monetary policy as he did. However, the fundamental transformation happened within Brazil. Murtinho's appointment shows that the preferences among the ruling elite changed once the country pacified.

The Funding Loan benefited Rothschilds. It prevented a default, maintaining the bank's reputation. Besides, the house gained £186,000 with the appreciation of the Brazilian bonds it held.[51] For Brazil, the new policy was economically severe but effective regarding payment capacity. The tight monetary policy appreciated the *mil-réis* by 66% between 1898 and 1903 (IBGE 1990, 593). The revenue from coffee exports fell in that currency, resulting in a deep recession and a spike in non-performing loans in the sector, which led to a series of bank runs in São Paulo (Triner 2000, 47; Hanley 2005, 172–75). Yet the measures solved the debt crisis, for the appreciation of the exchange rate and the introduction of a gold-tax on imports reduced the cost of the sovereign debt vis-à-vis taxation.

Fritsch (1988, 7) argues that officials did not understand the full extent of the adverse impacts of tight monetary policy on economic activity. Abreu (2002, 523–24) documents the political opposition to the Funding Loan in Brazil. Nevertheless, the policymakers had a good reason to implement orthodox policies: It improved credit conditions, which enabled further loans in the 1900s. A new cycle of lending started already in 1901, when the Campos Sales administration borrowed £17 million to invest in railways. In total, the government issued loans for £59 million in the 1900s, more than doubling the sovereign debt stock, which was worth £44.4 million at the beginning of the decade.[52] The state of São Paulo also borrowed extensively in those years—Chapter 5 will show that foreign credit financed the building of coffee stocks designed to sustain prices.

[51] *RA* I/000/77/4–5.

[52] Bouças (1955, 209).

The Orthodox monetary policy was a price the coffee growers paid to keep Brazil creditworthy right when the PRP established its hegemony over national politics. The oligarchy of São Paulo was going to rule the country in association with other regional elites until 1930. Pacification raised the costs of defaulting: Not committing to the Funding Loan in 1898 would have implied the collapse of foreign credit at the launching of that new national order.

Conclusion

Brazil ran war finance for most of the 1890s. The government would not consolidate its accounts because that policy entailed political penalties that were too high. An imminent default was a real threat to Rothschilds' premier status. Both government and bank were in weak positions, but Brazil had the upper hand while politics were unstable. Rothschilds' reputation would have made it strong in normal circumstances, but it debilitated the bank given its exposure to Brazil and the government's incapacity to pay. Rothschilds had no option but to accommodate the government's demands until the country pacified.

Brazil's fiscal accounts were still unsound in the late 1890s, but by then the government had the political capacity and strong incentives to improve it. Peace increased the cost of defaulting, which levelled out the balance between the government and the bank, allowing the latter to condition a rescue loan on orthodox economic policy. The Funding Loan is a case of shared policy ownership rather than policy imposition. Stakes were high for both players: A default would have destroyed Rothschilds' premier reputation and Brazil's clean payment record right when the ruling elite was establishing a stable oligarchic regime. The interests of the bank and the government converged around unpopular policies designed to recover payment capacity.

References

Archival Sources

BHMF Biblioteca Histórica do Ministério da Fazenda, Rio de Janeiro.
Contractos dos empréstimos em libras esterlinas do Governo Federal, 1883 a 1927, 332/225.
Funding Loan, Acordo do Brasil realizado pelo Governo Dr. Prudente de Moraes em 15 de Junho de 1898, 332/532.

IHGB Instituto Histórico e Geográfico Brasileiro, Rio de Janeiro.
Private Correspondence.
RA Rothschild Archive, London.
Ledger Balance, I.
Correspondence, XI.

Official and Contemporary Sources

Annual Report of the Council of the Corporation of Foreign Bondholders.

Barbosa, Ruy. 1892. *Finanças e política da República: discursos e escriptos.* Rio de Janeiro: Senado Federal.

Brasil, *Balanço da receita e despeza da República.* Rio de Janeiro: Imprensa Nacional.

Bouças, Valentim F. 1955. *Finanças do Brasil: dívida externa—1824–1945.* Rio de Janeiro: Ministério da Fazenda.

IBGE. 1990. *Estatísticas históricas do Brasil: séries econômicas, demográficas e sociais de 1550 a 1988.* Rio de Janeiro: Instituto Brasileiro de Geografia e Estatística.

The Economist.

The Investor's Monthly Manual.

The Times.

Secondary Sources

Abreu, Marcelo de Paiva. 2002. "Os Funding loans brasileiros—1898–1931." *Pesquisa e Planejamento Econômico* 32 (3):515–40.

Bacha, Edmar L., and Robert Greenhill. 1993. *150 anos de café.* São Paulo: Salamandra Consultoria Editorial.

Carvalho, José M. 1988. *Teatro de sombras: a política imperial.* Rio de Janeiro: IUPERJ.

———. 2005. *Forças armadas e política no Brasil.* São Paulo: Zahar.

Carvalho, Ney O. R. 2003. *O Encilhamento: anatomia de uma bolha brasileira.* São Paulo: Bovespa.

Catão, Luís A. V. 1992. "A New Wholesale Price Index for Brazil during the Period 1870–1913." *Revista Brasileira de Economia* 46 (4):519–34.

Costa, Emília V. 1998. *Da monarquia à república: momentos decisivos.* São Paulo: UNESP.

Fausto, Boris. 2007. "O sistema oligárquico nos primeiros anos da República." In *História geral da civilização brasileira: estrutura de poder e economia, 1889–1930*, edited by Fausto Boris, 17–171. Rio de Janeiro: Bertrand Brasil.

Ferguson, Niall. 1998. *The World's Banker: The History of the House of Rothschild.* New York: Weidenfeld & Nicolson.

Fishlow, Albert. 1995. "Latin American Nineteenth Century Public Debt: Theory and Practice." In *La Deuda Pública En América Latina En Perspectiva Histórica*, edited by Liehr Reinhard, 23–32. Madrid: Iberoamericana.

Flandreau, Marc, and Juan H. Flores. 2010. "Hamlet Without the Prince of Denmark: Relationship Banking and Conditionality Lending in the London Market For Foreign Government Debt, 1815-1913." IHEID Working Papers 08-2010. Economics Section, The Graduate Institute of International Studies.

Flandreau, Marc, and Frédéric Zumer. 2004. *The Making of Global Finance 1880–1913.* Paris: OECD.

Franco, Gustavo H. B. 1983. *Reforma monetária e instabilidade durante a transição republicana.* Rio de Janeiro: BNDES.

———. 2014. "A Primeira década republicana." In *A Ordem Do Progresso: Cem Anos de Política Econômica Republicana*, edited by Abreu, Marcelo P., Campus, 29–44. Rio de Janeiro.

Fritsch, Winston. 1988. *External Constraints on Economic Policy in Brazil, 1889–1930.* Houndmills: MacMillan.

Furtado, Celso. 2007. *Formação econômica do Brasil.* São Paulo: Companhia das Letras.

Graham, Richard. 1977. "Government Expenditures and Political Change in Brazil, 1880–1899: Who Got What." *Journal of Interamerican Studies and World Affairs* 19 (3):339–68.

Hanley, Anne G. 2005. *Native Capital: Financial Institutions and Economic Development in São Paulo, Brazil, 1850–1920.* Stanford: Stanford University Press.

Love, Joseph L. 1994. "Autonomia e interdependência: São Paulo e a Federação Brasileira, 1889–1937." In *História do Brasil*, edited by Boris Fausto, 58–83. São Paulo: EdUSP.

Mauro, Paolo, Nathan Sussman, and Yishay Yafeh. 2006. *Emerging Markets and Financial Globalization: Sovereign Bond Spreads in 1870–1913 and Today.* Oxford: Oxford University Press.

Meade, Teresa. 1989. "'Living Worse and Costing More': Resistance and Riot in Rio de Janeiro, 1890–1917." *Journal of Latin American Studies* 21 (2):241–66.

Mitchener, Kris J., and Marc D. Weidenmier. 2008. "The Baring Crisis and the Great Latin American Meltdown of the 1890s." *The Journal of Economic History* 68 (2):462–500.

Moniz, Edmundo. 1987. *Canudos: a guerra social.* São Paulo: Elo Editora.

Peláez, Carlos M., and Wilson Suzigan. 1981. *História monetária do Brasil.* Brasília: Editora Universidade de Brasília.

Queiroz, Suely R. 1986. *Os radicais da República: jacobinismo, ideologia e ação, 1893–1897.* São Paulo: Brasiliense.

Reverbel, Carlos. 1985. *Maragatos e pica-paus: guerra civil e degola no Rio Grande.* Porto Alegre: L&PM Editores.

Schulz, John. 1994. *O Exército na política: origens da intervenção militar, 1850–1894.* São Paulo: EdUSP.

———. 1996. *A crise financeira da abolição, 1875–1901.* São Paulo: EdUSP.

Summerhill, William R. 2015. *Inglorious Revolution: Political Institutions, Sovereign Debt, and Financial Underdevelopment in Imperial Brazil.* New Haven: Yale University Press.

Topik, Steven C. 1999. "Coffee." In *The Second Conquest of Latin America: Coffee, Henequen, and Oil During the Export Boom, 1850–1930*, edited by Steven C. Topik and Allen Wells, 34–72. Austin: University of Texas Press.

———. 2000. *Trade and Gunboats: The United States and Brazil in the Age of Empire.* Stanford: Stanford University Press.

———. 2014. *The Political Economy of the Brazilian State, 1889–1930.* Austin: University of Texas Press.

Triner, Gail. 2000. *Banking and Economic Development: Brazil, 1889–1930.* London: Palgrave Macmillan.

Weller, Leonardo. 2015. "Rothschilds' 'Delicate and Difficult Task': Reputation, Political Instability, and the Brazilian Rescue Loans of the 1890s." *Enterprise & Society* 16 (2): 381–412.

CHAPTER 5

Rothschilds and Coffee Finance: Brazil, 1898–1914

Brazil recovered from the 1890s debt crisis and re-established a reputation in the 1900s. The orthodox policies that followed the Funding Loan appreciated the *mil-réis* and strenghtened fiscal accounts. The arrangement penalised the coffee sector, which had to deal with the adverse effects of a strong exchange rate as well as falling coffee prices. The response came in the form of a stockpiling programme. The government of São Paulo borrowed abroad to finance massive purchases of coffee. The *Paulistas* also pressured the federal government to peg the *mil-réis* to gold at a depreciated rate, a rather peculiar form of Gold Standard that prevented the currency from becoming too strong. Rothschilds publicly opposed the manipulation of coffee prices but secretly supported the programme by transferring funds to the state of São Paulo.

The coffee scheme successfully sustained prices, while the late 1900s rubber boom expanded Brazilian exports. The balance of payments was positive, the monetary authority printed money to maintain the exchange rate stable, and Brazilian risk fell considerably. It was under these favourable conditions that the Brazilians broke Rothschilds' five-decade-old monopoly. The government issued loans in Paris between 1908 and 1911 through banks that charged lower commission.

Matters changed as coffee and rubber prices fell in the early 1910s, which triggered capital outflow and forced the government to reduce monetary stock to protect the gold parity. The government finally depreciated the exchange rate in 1914, when Rothschilds arranged the Second Funding Loan. Similar to the first Funding Loan, this new

L. Weller, *Sovereign Debt Crises and Negotiations in Brazil and Mexico, 1888-1914*, https://doi.org/10.1007/978-3-319-73633-4_5

operation included the issuing of bonds below the market rate, with which the government paid interests on most of the senior debt for three years. The arrangement also suspended amortisation of previously issued debt. However, the bank did not impose policy conditions, in contrast to the homonious rescue loan of 1898. This chapter assesses why the bank agreed upon such a generous package. It shows that the government pressured Rothschilds for a rescue loan, as it had done sixteen years before, but now the creditors understood that the crisis was cyclical rather than structural.

The Republic Borrows Again

Campos Sales administration (1898–1902) marks the beginning of the three-decade-long period during which Brazil was under a stable oligarchic regime. Regional parties dominated national politics. Besides the PRP, from São Paulo, the major parties were, in this order, the Partido Republicano Mineiro (PRM), from Minas Gerais, the most populous state in the federation, and the Partido Republicano Rio-Grandense (PRR), from the strategic Rio Grande do Sul. PRP and PRM controlled the executive: Out of the seven presidents in office from 1894 to 1914, three were *Paulistas* and two were *Mineiros*. At the base of the system, local leaders, most of whom were plantation owners, controlled elections and guaranteed votes for their governors in exchange for political privilege. The governors supported their respective political parties and the national government at the local level. Finally, the president of Congress had the prerogative of rejecting candidatures for the house, which prevented forces that opposed the regional elites from disturbing the oligarchic order (Trevisan 2001; Viscardi 2001).

Nevertheless, the political system was more complex and flexible than the simple coalition of the elites from the two larger states. The oligarchy from Rio Grande do Sul and the Army played a pivotal role between the major parties PRP and PRM. This became clear in 1909, when these two groups associated with Minas Gerais to form the Conservative Republican Party (PCR). Although short-lived, the PCR was the only important national party since the monarchy. It supported the candidature of Marshal Hermes da Fonseca (1910–1914), who won a disputed election against the PRP-backed candidate Ruy Barbosa (Fausto 2006, 256–72). Local elites from the Northeast were also relevant. They composed coalitions and demanded public funds in return (Graham 1977,

340–41). Until the more turbulent 1920s, several popular revolts—from lower rank Navy uprisings to industrial strikes—did not disturb the status quo.

Political stability changed the payoffs of the government when running economic policy and repaying the sovereign debt, as discussed in Chapter 2. Officials that govern stable regimes tend to be long-sighted, in opposition to those that face the imminent threats of wars and revolutions (Ozler and Tabellini 1991). That explains the contrast between the administrations of Prudente de Morais (1894–1898) and Campos Sales (1898–1902): The former printed money to fight wars, while the latter implemented the orthodox policies arranged under the Funding Loan. Sales government burned paper money and the national currency appreciated by 61% during his presidency. The Funding Loan also conditioned an increase in taxation, which contributed to the quick improvement in fiscal accounts: The government ran a surplus for most of the 1900s, starting already in 1903.

Brazilian risk fell sharply after the Funding Loan. It decreased from 7.2% to 3.5% between mid-1898 and 1901, when the government resumed paying services with cash. That was the same level Brazilian risk was in 1891, at the beginning of the turbulent first republican decade.[1] The British press published positive reports on Brazil, praising the government's commitment to orthodox policy. *The Investor's Monthly Manual* (n. 5, vol. 31, 31 May 1901, p. 225) stated that Brazil "can experience no difficulty in maintaining payments regularly," and *The Investor's Review* printed that "matters appear to have improved wonderfully for the Republic (…) and the condition of affairs (…) undoubtedly breeds encouragement for the future."[2] Brazilian risk continued to fall, reaching 2% in 1905 and 1.5% in 1910.

As credit costs fell, Brazil borrowed. The government issued a £16.6 loan already in 1901 to nationalise railways. The government had guaranteed the profitability of private railway companies, which underperformed during the economic crisis that followed the Funding Loan. The nationalization programme liberated the government from meeting new profit guarantees, contributing for the improvement of fiscal accounts. A new loan issued in 1903 financed public works in Rio de Janeiro, including a new port and modern avenues and squares. The government

[1] See Fig. 1.1.

[2] *The Investor's Review*, 22 June 1901, vol. 16, p. 780.

borrowed 12% more in those two years than it had done in the 1890s altogether. Brazil continued to borrow heavily until the First World War, issuing 11 further loans. In total, the borrowing totalled £91 million between 1901 and 1914. At current prices, that was about half of what the government (both imperial and federal) had borrowed since its first loan in 1824.

The credit improvement was consistent with the *Belle Époque*: The coefficient of correlation between Brazilian risk and the average risk of emergent countries was 0.95 between 1901 and 1913. Yet the former decreased on average 5.64% per year, while the latter reduced by an annual average of 1.45%.[3] The world market was favourable for an improvement in credit, but Brazil over-performed the market because it was cashing out the results of the orthodox policies that restored its reputation as the best borrower in Latin America.[4]

Brazil Suspends Rothschilds' Monopoly

The government broke Rothschilds' monopoly when it issued four loans in Paris through French banks—Societe Généràl, Paribas, Crédit Mobilier and Caisse Comercialle—between 1909 and 1911. The loans were part of the inflow of French capital in Brazil in the 1900s, which included private companies and municipal debt (Abreu 1993). The government borrowed in Paris to pay lower commission. The contracts of the 1908, 1909 and 1910 loans do not mention commission, most probably because the underwriters did not charge it. The latter contract states that the underwriter (Crédit Mobilier) was supposed to pay for all the costs of the loan, except for the printing of bonds, the only expenditure the government covered.[5] The 1911 contract is the only one that contains figures on commission: 0.75% on issuing and 0.5% on redemption.[6] This is substantially less than what Brazil paid Rothschilds. In 1908, that bank charged upfront 1.75% on issuing, 1.25% on brokerage, and

[3] Calculated from *The Investor's Monthly Manual*. See Chapter 4 for more on this emergent index.

[4] The risk premium of Brazil in the 1900s was below that paid by Argentina, Chile and Mexico in this order. Calculated from *The Investor's Monthly Manual*.

[5] *BHMF* 332/226.

[6] Ibid., Empréstimo de 1911.

1.25% on the underwriting of that year's loan.[7] Rothschilds' commission increased slightly in 1911, when it charged a total of 4.5%.[8]

In contrast to Rothschilds, the French banks took the bonds in firm—they held them instead of passing them on to the final bondholders at the issuing price. Instead of charging commission, the bankers expected to gain from the sale of bonds at a higher price on the secondary market, a business that depended on price variations and thus involved risk. Yet the loans were issued at slightly lower risk premium than those Rothschilds underwrote in that same period.[9] As contenders, the French banks needed to offer good conditions to convince Brazil to depart from its exclusive association with the world's top bank.

The managers of Rothschilds were of course not pleased to see the end of their profitable monopoly. In 1908, Alfred Rothschild wrote to his French cousin that "Société Genéral has absolutely no right to pretend that they are the financial Representatives of Brasil in France." But the banker did not appear to be surprised. He wrote that "Brazilian finance and public work in that huge country are in somewhat peculiar position just now (…) various banks in the continent are all as you yourself say anxious for new business."[10] The French banks wanted a slice of Rothschilds' exclusive and attractive Brazilian enterprise, and the government took advantage of that demand. Rothschilds did not retaliate by suspending relation: It continued to underwrite loans after 1908. It seems that Brazil was so "huge" that there was plenty of space for everyone. Alfred Rothschild recognised that:

> The Country is quite prosperous in fact more than prosperous. There are £15 million Gold in the Caisse de Conversion, the Coffee crop has yield much more money than was expected and the Cocoa and Rubber crops are bringing in millions. The amount of rubber sold realised £5 million, this year the Coffee will be worth more than £20 million, nearly £25 million, and thanks to the outcry about share grown cocoa, Pernambuco is securing a great and ready market for its chief commodity on Stock Exchange.[11]

[7] *BHMF* 332/225, Empréstimo de 1908, section VI.

[8] Ibid., Empréstimo de 1911, section VI.

[9] See Table 1.1.

[10] *RA* Alfred Rothschild to Gustave Rothschild, 26 May 1908, XI/130A/219080526.

[11] *RA* Alfred Rothschild to Gustave Rothschild, 21 February 1910, XI/130A/4 19100221.

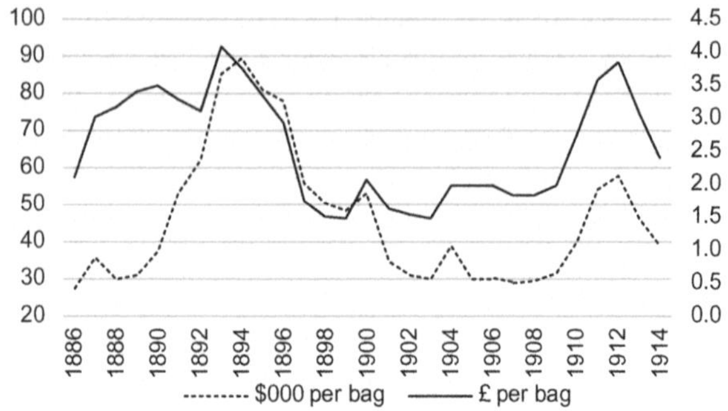

Fig. 5.1 Coffee price in Rio de Janeiro, 1886–1914 (1$000 and £ per bag) (*Source* IBGE (1990, 312, 591, 593). *Note Mil-réis* on the left-hand axis and British pounds on the right-hand axis)

Prosperity and reputation took Brazil to Paris, and Rothschilds did nothing but to grumble in private.

The Coffee Lobby

The supply of coffee is inelastic: A coffee tree takes about five years to start producing beans and yield peaks when it is over a decade old. Farmers invested in new groves in the late 1880s and early 1890s, when prices were high and immigration soared. Output grew by the turn of the century, after which the international market remained in a state of chronic oversupply. Brazil was the largest producer in the world, with over three quarters of global supply in the 1900s (Bacha and Greenhill 1993, 308, 313). The growth of Brazilian output was enough to depress international prices. Differently from the 1890s, when a weak *mil-réis* protected the sector from falling external prices, the orthodox policies arranged under the Funding Loan strengthened the currency and squeezed profitability. Figure 5.1 shows the price of coffee in both *mil-réis* and British pounds. The former increased in the early 1890s, when monetary expansion depreciated the exchange rate. Ten years later, in contrast, exchange rate appreciation reduced the price in *mil-réis* more than in pounds.

Signs of a record crop in 1906 pushed the government of São Paulo to launch initiatives that shaped national policies for the rest of the decade. The most remarkable of those ventures was the coffee valorisation scheme, which promoted stockpiling to stabilise prices worldwide. Highly experimental, the programme constituted in the first initiative to control commodity prices at a global level (Topik 1999, 67–69). The state government borrowed £1 million from Disconto Gesellschaft, the underwriters of the "coffee bonds." The funds financed the purchase of stocks, which were mostly held in European and US ports to guarantee the loan.

São Paulo's Governor Jorge Piratininga (1904–1908) requested the federal government to back the coffee bonds, which President (and former governor of São Paulo and finance minister) Rodrigues Alves (1902–1906) refused to do. Alves considered that the programme conflicted with his administration's orthodox orientation (Peláez 1971, 56). The president was in line with Rothschilds, whose directors referred to the scheme as an "impossible speculation" and the "most dangerous and suicidal policy."[12] Privately, the bankers established that they would "do our best to impress upon the Government and the President how suicidal it would be on their part to support a reckless speculative scheme which can but end in a collapse."[13]

The 1906–1907 harvest was so abundant that São Paulo needed more funds to prevent the price of coffee from falling. It borrowed extra £3 million through the London-based financier Henry Schroeder (Peláez 1971, 74). Output increased even more in the following year, bringing the scheme to the edge of collapsing. Stocks totalled 2.6 million bags in 1906, which corresponded to 19% of that year's exports. By late 1907, stocks reached 8 million bags, the equivalent of 27% of exports in both years.[14] The government of São Paulo did not find a banker that would underwrite more coffee bonds, and the federal administration transferred the funds the state needed to continue stocking coffee.

Not much information is available on that unofficial operation, yet some data appear in a letter President Afonso Pena (1906–1909) sent

[12] *RA* Rothschilds to Minister Campista, 14 February 1907, XI/142/1905–1907. This point appears in Holloway (1975).

[13] *RA* Alfred Rothschild (London) to Gustave Rothschilds (Paris), 7 August 1906, XI.130A/0/19060807.

[14] Calculated from Peláez (1971, 74–75) and IBGE (1990, 591, 593).

to his predecessor Rodrigues Alves. Pena stated that the "government of São Paulo has asked £3 million in federal aid."[15] The president mentioned a "colossal loan" that made "Mrss. Rothschilds rush to offer their services."[16] However, the government suspended the operation because of the world financial crisis of 1907. President Pena then declared that "in such case, I will use part of the resources available from the huge increase in (tax) revenue" and funds "held by our financial agents, including moneys to the improvement of (Rio de Janeiro's) Harbour."[17]

It is not clear why the federal government decided to rescue São Paulo, a question that remains unanswered in the secondary literature. Perhaps the operation became more likely after the orthodox-minded Rodrigues Alves stepped down in 1906. The only point that seems to be clear from the letter quoted above is that a significant share of the resources came from the account the federal government had with Rothschilds. The account registered £5.4 million in mid-1904, just after the government had issued a loan to finance the construction of the docks mentioned in the correspondence.[18] The balance then rose to £6.1 million in 1906 (the year when São Paulo launched the valorisation scheme), but fell to £4.6 million in 1907 and to only £1.7 in the following year.[19] Meanwhile, Alfred Rothschild informed his relatives that "the Brazilian Government has already advanced to the State of San Paulo £1,200,000." [20]

The bankers "did not wish to identify ourselves with this scheme"[21], but they nevertheless agreed to participate in the bailing-out of São Paulo. A default on the coffee bonds would have caused a crisis in Brazil, depressing the quotation of all the country's securities. The importance

[15] *ANB* Afonso Pena to Rodrigues Alves, 23 September 1907, *Coleção Afonso Pena*, box 5, n. 11.48.

[16] Ibid.

[17] Ibid.

[18] *RA* I/000/77/5.

[19] *RA* I/000/77/5.

[20] *RA* Alfred Rothschild to Gustave Rothschild, 1 January 1907, XI/130A/19071001.

[21] *RA* Alfred Rothschild to Gustave Rothschild, 20 February 1907, XI/130A/1 19070220.

of São Paulo in the federation and Rothschilds' exposure to Brazil forced the bankers to play a role they did not wish.

The coffee valorisation scheme was a success. Stocks prevent the large harvest of 1906–1907 from depressing prices below the record low of 1903. Figure 5.1 shows that prices started to increase in 1908 and reached a maximum in 1910, when São Paulo sold the stocks at a profit and redeemed the coffee bonds. The timing was fortunate: Three years later, a New York court condemned the scheme based on the anti-cartel legislation and ordered the seizure of the stocks held in the city, but by then the coffee had been already sold. However, the case made it impossible for São Paulo or the federal government to launch a new stockpiling programme involving capital from the USA.

Brazil's Unorthodox Gold Standard

Brazil joined the Gold Standard in 1907, around the same time the government of São Paulo started to intervene in the coffee market. The two policies were strongly connected. The stockpiling programme would increase coffee prices and thus the revenue from exports. The state government borrowed abroad to finance the scheme, which also accounted for an inflow of hard currency. Together, these two consequences of the coffee programme would appreciate the *mil-réis* and reduce the profitability of the coffee sectors—precisely what the scheme intended to avoid. The rapid growth of rubber exports flowing from the Amazon region and the federal government's loans also contributed to the strengthening of the national currency. The currency appreciated by one-third between 1903 and 1906. Without a policy designed to stop the exchange rate from appreciating even further, the country's positive external accounts would have penalised the coffee sector in spite of São Paulo's effort in reducing the supply of that product on the world market (Topik 1999, 71; Holloway 1975, 69–74; Peláez 1971, 9).

The *Paulistas* pressured the federal government to launch a *caisse* of conversion, which worked similarly to a currency board in establishing an exchange rate peg. The government deposited the foreign exchange flowing into the country in the *caisse* and printed domestic money accordingly, at the rate of 15 pence per *mil-réis*. That was lower than the current market exchange rate, which fluctuated around 16 in 1907 (Fritsch 1988, 14–15). Brazil's Gold Standard was peculiar: It was sat up to depreciate (rather than to appreciate) the national currency (Peláez

Table 5.1 Brazil's financial data, 1898–1914 (*Source* IBGE (1990, 312, 541–42, 591–99) for monetary growth, coffee price and exchange rate; Balanço da receita e despeza da República, and IBGE (1990, 617–18) for primary surplus; Bouças (1955, 220) for sovereign debt services)

	Monetary growth (M_2, %)	*Exchange rate (pense/ mil-réis)*	*Primary surplus*		*Sovereign debt service (£ million)*	*SD service (% tax revenue)*
			EHB (£ million)	*Official (£ million)*		
1899	−2.41	7.42	3.45	3.45	0.22	2.18
1900	−10.27	9.43	−1.33	−0.23	0.36	2.97
1901	−22.39	11.33	1.94	1.78	1.97	13.68
1902	−1.95	11.94	5.97	3.86	1.92	11.23
1903	−2.23	11.99	5.97	5.75	1.92	9.23
1904	4.62	12.24	2.64	2.38	1.92	8.49
1905	3.21	15.94	6.12	3.35	2.09	7.83
1906	1.89	16.19	4.94	−0.90	2.09	7.17
1907	15.51	15.24	5.13	−1.82	2.09	6.13
1908	1.22	15.16	−0.32	−3.74	2.34	8.39
1909	9.04	15.14	0.85	−1.90	3.04	10.71
1910	21.51	16.27	−1.02	−3.49	2.99	8.41
1911	9.82	16.12	−1.92	−6.72	3.59	9.48
1912	10.69	16.16	−5.51	−12.17	3.99	9.63
1913	−2.89	16.11	0.03	−8.54	4.27	9.72
1914	−8.36	14.85	−14.92	−11.76	4.05	15.46

and Suzigan 1981, 40–41). In contrast to what one would expect from the literature on the classic Gold Standard, the Brazilian version of that policy allowed the government to print money. Table 5.1 shows that the monetary stock increased in 1907.

Exports decreased during the world crisis of 1908, and the government momentarily reduced the growth in monetary stock. The trade crisis depressed customs revenue, and the government ran a deficit, which was going to increase in the following years. External accounts recovered quickly, however. The revenue from rubber peaked in the late 1900s, when that commodity became as important as coffee in national exports. The development of more efficient rubber plantations in Southeast Asia burst the rubber boom and prices collapsed by half in 1911 (IBGE

1990, 309).[22] Coffee prices were high in those years, which compensated for the collapse of the rubber economy. This commodity lottery permitted the government to continue expanding the monetary stock in the first years of the 1910s.

The government printed money to defend the peg. The policy increased liquidity and helped the Brazilian market to absolve public domestic bonds, which the government issued to finance the fiscal deficit. The data on the domestic debt are unprecise, but the federal budget reported figures on its services, which increased by an average of 12% per year between 1908, when fiscal accounts started to deteriorate, and 1913. The services on the domestic debt were equivalent to about 7% of tax revenue during that period.[23] In short, the combination of favourable external accounts and the *caisse* of conversion helped the government to fund the deficit.

Fiscal policy became even more unsound during the presidency of Marshal Hermes da Fonseca (1910–1914). A prestigious high-rank military, Fonseca intended to centralise power in the hands of the federal government and increase the role of the state in the economy. His administration invested in public works, subsidised the building of railways and raised the defence budget (Silva and Carneiro 1983). The deficit increased from the equivalent of 15% of tax revenue in 1909 to 81% in 1914, when Fonseca stepped down (IBGE 1990, 616–18). According to the official data, the primary fiscal balance was already lower than the services due on the sovereign debt in 1906. Although more optimistic, the reconstructed series show that the government ran a primary deficit in 1908. From then on, both series reflect the rapid deterioration of fiscal accounts, with primary balance deep in the red.[24]

The exchange rate peg conditioned a pro-cyclical economic policy. Positive external accounts allowed the government to run lose fiscal and monetary policies, which speeded up economic growth. The booming economy attracted foreign exchange in the form of international investments and credit in banking, trade and railways. Balance of Payments results were so positive in 1910 that the *caisse* accumulated £20 million in foreign exchange reserves and the government appreciated the peg

[22] See Dean (2002, 53–54) for more on the rubber boom.

[23] *Balanço da Receita e Despeza da República*, and IBGE (1990, 616–18).

[24] See Table 5.1.

rate from 15 to 16 *mil-réis* to pence. It was not a surprise that the country was able to borrow £10 million at 4% in that year, in an operation that converted the old 5 per cent-type debt. Conditions were favourable, from economic activity to credit rate, but only as long as the revenue from exports continued to rise.

Another Debt Crisis

The exchange rate peg speeded up economic growth in good times but also deepened a recession when coffee prices started falling in 1913 (Fritsch 1988, 18). Years of state protection stimulated farmers to invest in new grooves, increasing oversupply in the long run. São Paulo found it impossible to launch a new stockpiling programme when a good harvest reduced world prices. Oversupply was too large, and the US financial market was closed to a second scheme. The revenue from exports fell by 28% between 1913 and 1914, and Brazil ran a trade deficit for the first time in five decades (IBGE 1987, 569–70, 616). The monetary authorities responded to the deterioration in external accounts by selling foreign exchange reserves and reducing liquidity. M_2 shrank by 13% from early 1913 to mid-1914, when the government dumped the *caisse* and allowed the exchange rate to depreciate.

Brazilian risk increased from an average of 1.54% in 1912 to 2.44% in the first half of 1914, which had no parallel among other borrowing countries—with the exception of revolutionary Mexico, the topic of Chapter 8. The coefficient of correlation between Brazilian risk and the average emergent risk excluding Brazil is 0.48 between January 1912 and June 1914, against 0.88 since the beginning of the century up to 1911. The correlation is only 0.18 in 1912–1914 if Mexico is excluded from the sample.[25] The Brazilian and Mexican crises responded for most of the deterioration of the credit available on the market in the years that preceded the First World War.

Rothschilds sent a representative to Brazil in late 1912. The agent "had several interviews with the Finance Minister and impressed upon him the necessity of avoiding constant small guarantees issues for the various Railways and other public works."[26] The bankers understood that it was time for the Fonseca administration to retrench expenditure. The

[25] Calculated from *The Investor's Monthly Manual*.

[26] *RA* Alfred Rothschild to Gustave Rothschild, 22 October 1912, XI/130A/6A.

Finance Minister assured the bank "that he is doing his best to prevent these large deficits by a policy of retrenchment" and that his government "does not intend to give any more guarantees in connection with Railway or any other commercial or industrial enterprise."[27]

The government did attempt to consolidate fiscal accounts. Expenditure fell by 13% between 1912 and 1914 according to official data, and by 3% if the more accurate re-constructed data are considered. That was insufficient, for tax revenue collapsed by 29% according to both sources. The deterioration of external accounts and the recession reduced imports, from which the government raised almost half of its tax revenue. A shrinking tax base compromised the government's effort to improve payment capacity, leaving officials with no alternative but to borrow to pay the services due on the sovereign debt. Instead of investing in productive enterprises, as it had done in the previous decade, Brazil was now about to issue a new loan to avoid a default.

Rothschilds bought £3.2 million in Brazilian treasury notes that were due in 1913. The bank then underwrote a new long-term loan to redeem those bills and to cover others obligations that also matured in that year. The bonds were 5 instead of 4 per cent-type, reflecting the deterioration in credit conditions. Minister Francisco Sales (1910–1913) established a lower bound for the discount rate at 97%. Alfred Rothschild described the minister as "most pathetic (and) in fact quite sentimental," but in the end he agreed on that rate.[28] The 1913 loan was issued in May at a 1.84% risk premium, which was precisely the Brazilian risk in that month, but below the rate of the following months: Brazilian risk increased to 1.91% and 1.99% in June and July, respectively.[29]

In an official letter to the finance minister, Rothschilds complained that "the public subscription is not at all up to expectation, the loan being quoted at a discount which prevents the public from subscribing, the amount being considered too large and the price high."[30] Taking a similar view, *The Economist* referred to the "unfavourable reception given

[27] *RA* Rothschilds to Brazilian Minister Sales, 21 October 1912, XI/142.

[28] *RA* Alfred Rothschild to Gustave Rothschilds, 28 April 1913, XI/130A/6A.

[29] See Fig. 1.1.

[30] *RA* Rothschilds to Minister Sales, 6 May 1913, XI/65/13.

in London to the new Brazilian loan."[31] The bankers described the operation as a "herculean task (that) no House except ourselves could have underwritten and accomplished."[32] Rothschilds took £366,880 of the bonds. That seemed to have influenced the market, which in the end provided the credit the government needed.[33]

Brazil would have been short of funds without Rothschilds, but the government still had some leverage to negotiate. Besides exposure to Brazil, the bankers accommodated its client's demand because they understood that the crisis was cyclical. They wrote to the finance minister that "we may look forward to a gradual improvement in the financial and commercial market and if our hopes are realised the demand for the produce of Brazil will no doubt increase."[34] The sanguine position of the bankers also appears in the following passage:

> It is highly necessary for the Brazilian Government to be wise, economical and cautious. I am certain that they realize this themselves, that they will endeavour considerably to reduce their expenditure and they will not raise any fresh loans if they can. (...) you must not blame the Government too much.[35]

Differently from the 1890s, when political instability had deteriorated payment capacity *before* coffee prices began to fall, in the 1910s an unusual Gold Standard had allowed the government to run lose economic policy *until* coffee prices collapsed. In the 1890s, Rothschilds had to wait for the country to pacify to pressure for the tightening of monetary policy. In the 1910s, the bank provided credit to hold its client through a circumstantial crisis. Brazil faced a liquidity rather than a structural crisis, and Rothschilds was aware of that fact.

[31] *The Economist*, 10 May 1913, issue 3637, pp. 10, 11.

[32] *RA* Rothschilds to Minister Sales, 6 May 1913, XI/65/13.

[33] *RA* I/000/77/5.

[34] *RA* Rothschilds to Minister Corrêa, 28 July 1913, XI/65/13

[35] *RA* Alfred Rothschild to Gustave Rothschilds, 19 August 1913, XI/130A/6A

Rothschilds Rescues Again: The Second Funding Loan

Coffee prices continued to fall in 1914, and Brazil's urgent need of credit abridged Rothschilds' optimism. In early 1914, the new Finance Minister Rivadavia Corrêa (1913–1914) informed that the government had "no funds to meet (the) £5 Millions in respect of interest on the foreign loans" and could not "see where they are to come from."[36] The Brazilians were pressuring for another rescue loan, but Rothschilds was not willing to underwriter it: Alfred Rothschild considered a "Brazilian Operation quite out of the question."[37] He informed Minister Corrêa that "the English market is not well disposed for Brazilian Securities at the present moment."[38]

That does not mean that a rescue loan was out of question. A few months later, the banker "approached (...) friends and others who act with us (...) to find out what amount and on what conditions they would be prepared to purchase Brazilian Treasury Bills."[39] Rothschilds was buying time, waiting for an improvement in the coffee market or yet more expenditure cuts from the Brazilian government. This point appears in the following passage, wrote in a cable to minister Corrêa:

> Your Excellency mentions the large item of £5 Millions in respect of interest on the foreign loans and Your Excellency says at the same time that you have no funds to meet the same and other claims besides, nor do you see where they are to come from. Under these circumstances it is impossible for us to formulate any plan until we hear from you what steps you intend taking on your side in order to meet with these deficiencies because until we know that they are ample and efficacious it will be impossible for us to try and obtain money from the public until we can prove to them that you quite prepared to give fresh and ample new guarantees.[40]

Besides the market's lack of appetite for Brazilian securities, asymmetry of information also explains why the bankers were so cautious about another loan. Rothschilds no longer held a monopoly over Brazil's sovereign debt, and thus it did not have access to first-hand information on

[36] *RA* Rothschilds to Minister Corrêa, 17 April 1914, XI/65/13.

[37] *RA* Alfred Rothschild to Gustave Rothschild, 19 December 1913, XI/130A/6A.

[38] *RA* Alfred Rothschild to Minister Corrêa, 23 December 1913, XI/65/13.

[39] *RA* Alfred Rothschild to Minister Corrêa, 17 February 1914, XI/65/13.

[40] *RA* Alfred Rothschild to Minister Corrêa, 17 April 1914, XI/65/13.

the whole of the sovereign debt. Alfred Rothschild felt that "the present Finance Minister does not see exactly eye to eye with us," and therefore, their assessment about the payment capacity of the Brazilian government was "limited to the official data that is far from accurate."[41] In fact, the fiscal deficit of 1913 was the equivalent of £16 or £12 million depending on the sources—respectively the contemporary and reconstructed series.

Rothschilds requested information from the finance minister, including "the absolute amount required for internal and external debts, the total amounts of claims which the Delegate of the Treasury is yearly making on us in addition to other large claims made both here and on the Continent."[42] A month later the banker inquired about "the exact state of the Finance of the Government, the requirements of the service of the public debt and the acknowledged claims of Europeans creditors."[43] Without such pieces of information, Alfred Rothschild found it "impossible (…) to formulate a plan which would not only meet the exigencies of the moment but would likewise place Brazil credit again on a firm and solid basis."[44]

One last factor explains why Rothschilds was delaying the issuing of a rescue loan: It was attempting to form a large syndicate, including as many underwriters as possible. Alfred Rothschild wrote to his relatives in Paris that it "is absolutely necessary (that) there is absolutely no rivalry between London and Paris and that we are both acting together to regard the interest of Brazil and put the financial position on a really sound basis."[45] In the end, nearly every house that had underwritten Brazilian bonds participated in the Second Funding Loan. The syndicate included Société Général and Paribas, which underwrote Brazilian loans in Paris, and Disconto Gesellschaft, the underwriters of the coffee loans to São Paulo. The larger the syndicate, the smaller the Rothschilds' burden in the rescue loan.

Meanwhile, the Brazilians were negotiating the terms of the operation. In April 1914, the bank proposed a "£20 million loan at 5.5 percent interest and discounted at around 94 percent."[46] That resulted in

[41] *RA* Alfred Rothschild to Minister Corrêa, 24 March 1914, XI/65/13.

[42] *RA* Alfred Rothschild to Minister Corrêa, 23 February 1914, XI/65/13.

[43] *RA* Alfred Rothschild to Minister Corrêa, 17 March 1914, XI/65/13.

[44] *RA* Alfred Rothschild to Minister Corrêa, 23 February 1914, XI/65/13.

[45] *RA* London to Paris Rothschilds, 25 March 1914, XI/130A/6A.

[46] *RA* Rothschilds to Minister Corrêa, 27 April 1914, XI/65/13.

a 2.52% risk premium, slightly below Brazilian risk, which was 2.60%. The bankers imposed several conditions that resemble those requested when both parties negotiated the 1898 Funding Loan. In their words, Brazil was to agree to "pledge the Custom House receipts for the service of Interest and Sinking Fund on (A) the existing Brazilian Government Loans, and (B) a new loan to be issued (...)." What is more, "the Customs receipts shall not be further pledged to any other parties for any further operations either Treasury Bills or long-dated Loans." Finally, it was considered an "essential condition that the Government should lease at once the Central Railway"—the same company that was at the centre of the Funding Loan's negotiations sixteen years before.[47]

Finance minister Corrêa replied that the government was "unable to accept the terms" for political reasons.[48] The bankers expressed "regret (for) the long procrastinations which have taken place" and declared that "owing to the state of European politics the negotiations have to be suspended for the present." Nevertheless, Rothschilds' commitment to Brazil seems to have remained unshaken. They wrote in that same cable that "it is however needless to say that should the crisis pass over which we most ardently hope will be the case, the negotiations then would be resumed at once."[49]

The "crisis" Rothschild referred to was the outbreak of the First World War. By October 1914, it was already clear that the conflict was greater than the public had expected. International financial markets were depressed, and the cost of defaulting not borrowing again at the same rate—fell together with the bondholders' willingness of buying foreign debt. Brazil became more likely to suspend payments, turning its debt crisis into a greater threat for Rothschilds. The bankers then proposed a far more generous deal. They arranged that the syndicate would underwrite up to £15 million in bonds that would cover the interests due on the senior debt up to three years, with the 1903 loan as the only exception. The loan was cheap relative to market conditions—it was launched at a 1.67% risk premium, nearly half of Brazilian risk at the time. What is more, the government was free from paying amortizations in the following 13 years.[50] The new loan was similar to what had been

[47] Ibid.

[48] *RA* Minister Corrêa to Rothschilds, 7 July 1914, X/111/29.

[49] *RA* Rothschilds to Minister Corrêa, 27 July 1914, X/111/29.

[50] Calculated from *BHMF* 332/225, Bouças (1955, p. 254), and *The Investor's Monthly Manual*.

agreed in 1898, which explains why it was called the Second Funding Loan; but this time the government was not required to burn paper money or to introduce new taxes. The operation did not involve conditions on economic policy.

Conclusion

The comparison of the relative power between the Brazilian government and Rothschilds in 1898 and 1914 is enlightening. In both occasions, the government would not have been able to borrow the funds it needed through other underwriters. The bank was still highly exposed in 1914, when officials stressed the poor state of fiscal accounts to pressure for a generous loan, just like they had done in 1898. The crisis increased the government's relative power because of Rothschilds' exposure. The difference is that politics was still stabilizing in the late 1890s; by 1914, in contrast, the country had been peaceful for over a decade.

The understanding that the crisis was cyclical explains why Rothschilds did not include conditions in the Second Funding Loan. Perhaps the bankers expected to profit from the appreciation of Brazilian securities once coffee prices recovered. They were right ex-anti, but the duration and intensity of the First World War—not anticipated at the time—delayed that outcome. Coffee prices only recovered in 1919, and the Brazilian risk remained well above 1.85%—the risk premium at which the loan was issued—for the rest of the decade.[51] Yet the Second Funding Loan was a success because it prevented Brazil from defaulting. The government would only suspend payments in the 1930s, but by that time the Soviet moratorium on the Russian debt had long ruined Rothschilds' default-free brand.

References

Archival Sources

ANB Arquivo Nacional do Brasil, Rio de Janeiro.
Coleção Afonso Pena.

BHMF Biblioteca Histórica do Ministério da Fazenda, Rio de Janeiro.
Contractos dos empréstimos em libras esterlinas do Governo Federal, 1883 a 1927.

[51] Calculated from IBGE (1990, p. 571) and *The Investor's Monthly Manual*.

Contractos dos empréstimos em francos e em dollar do governo, 332/226.

RA Rothschild Archive, London.
Ledger Balance, I.
Correspondence, XI.

Official and Contemporary Sources

Brasil. *Balanço da receita e despeza da República.* Rio de Janeiro: Imprensa Nacional.

Bouças, Valentim F. 1955. *Finanças do Brasil: dívida externa—1824–1945.* Rio de Janeiro: Ministério da Fazenda.

IBGE. 1990. *Estatísticas históricas do Brasil: séries econômicas, demográficas e sociais de 1550 a 1988.* Rio de Janeiro: Instituto Brasileiro de Geografia e Estatística.

The Economist.

The Investor's Monthly Manual.

The Investor's Review.

The Times.

Secondary Sources

Abreu, Marcelo P. 1993. "A dívida pública externa brasileira em francos franceses, 1888–1956." Working Papers 305. Department of Economics PUC-Rio.

Bacha, Edmar L., and Robert Greenhill. 1993. *150 anos de café.* São Paulo: Salamandra Consultoria Editorial.

Dean, Warren. 2002. *Brazil and the Struggle for Rubber: A Study in Environmental History.* Cambridge: Cambridge University Press.

Fausto, Boris. 2006. *História geral da civilização brasileira. O Brasil republicano. sociedade e instituições. 1889–1930—Volume 9.* São Paulo: Bertrand.

Fritsch, Winston. 1988. *External Constraints on Economic Policy in Brazil, 1889–1930.* Houndmills: MacMillan.

Graham, Richard. 1977. "Government Expenditures and Political Change in Brazil, 1880–1899: Who Got What." *Journal of Interamerican Studies and World Affairs* 19 (3):339–68.

Holloway, Thomas H. 1975. *The Brazilian Coffee Valorization of 1906: Regional Politics and Economic Dependence.* Madison: University of Wisconsin.

Ozler, Sule, and Guido Tabellini. 1991. "External Debt and Political Instability." 582. CEPR Discussion Papers. C.E.P.R. Discussion Papers.

Peláez, Carlos M. 1971. "Análise econômica do programa brasileiro de sustentação do café—1906–1945: Teoria, política e medição." *Revista Brasileira de Economia* 25 (4):5–212.

Peláez, Carlos M., and Wilson Suzigan. 1981. *História monetária do Brasil.* Brasília: Editora Universidade de Brasília.

Silva, Hélio, and Maria C. R. Carneiro. 1983. *Hermes da Fonseca, um marechal na presidência, 1910–1914.* São Paulo: Grupo de Comunicação Três.

Topik, Steven C. 1999. "Coffee." In *The Second Conquest of Latin America: Coffee, Henequen, and Oil During the Export Boom, 1850–1930*, edited by Steven C. Topik and Allen Wells, 43-72. Austin: University of Texas Press.

Trevisan, Leonardo. 2001. *A República Velha.* São Paulo: Global Editora.

Viscardi, Cláudia M. R. 2001. *O teatro das oligarquias: uma revisão da 'política do café com leite'.* Belo Horizonte: C/Arte.

PART III

Mexico versus Mediocre Banks

CHAPTER 6

From Defaults to Redemption: Mexico, 1821–1890

Mexico was one of the world's worst borrowers. The government issued loans in London in the 1820s, only to default shortly afterwards. The debt remained unpaid for about six decades, during which the creditors, organised under the Committee of the Mexican Bondholders, imposed an embargo that prevented the state as well as domestic companies from floating bonds abroad. Mexico was a failed state, subject to many foreign invasions, civil wars and territorial losses. It borrowed in the 1860s during a French-backed monarchic regime. The monarchy did not last more than a few years and the new republican government repudiated its debt.

Matters started to change under the dictatorship of Porfirio Díaz (1876–1880, 1884–1911), who built an autocratic and centralised state that pacified the country and delivered economic growth. The government converted the old defaulted debt in 1885, at the start of Díaz's second (and very long) administration, and issued a new loan three years later. The revenue from that lending funded the redemption of the conversion bonds, clearing Mexico's record on the market. This chapter provides background on the history of the Mexican debt to explain why bankers decided to lend to a debt delinquent ruled by a dictator.

The financiers that arranged the 1888 loan already played a key role in Mexico's finance. They controlled Banamex, a semi-official bank that managed the government's accounts and held most of the domestic public debt. The syndicate used its influence to force Díaz to issue the bonds at expensive terms, which made the 1888 loan the most profitable of

L. Weller, *Sovereign Debt Crises and Negotiations in Brazil and Mexico, 1888-1914*, https://doi.org/10.1007/978-3-319-73633-4_6

the Porfiriato. The bankers intended to hold exclusivity over the country's debt, anticipating a series of loans that would follow the 1885 settlement. The government accepted bad borrowing terms to re-enter the market but refused to have a patron bank, borrowing from a different syndicate already in 1889. That choice liberated Mexico's negotiators to bargain for good borrowing conditions, which they would do with surprisingly good results, as will be shown in Chapter 7.

Wars, Invasions and Failed State

A politically polarised and unstable country emerged from Mexico's eleven-year-long war of independence. Between the 1821 and 1867—the dates of independence and the victory over the last foreign invasion, respectively—the country had on average two new administrations per year. As a consequence, Mexico lagged behind in railways, banking and trade even for Latin American standards. This section describes the political side of this narrative; next section analyses the impacts of instability on state finance and sovereign debt.

The first government of independent Mexico was the short-lived empire of Agustín de Iturbide (1822–1823). A supporter of Spain at the beginning of the war of independence, Iturbide changed sides to arrange a compromise between Mexican-born rebels and the Spanish-born elite of Mexico City. The latter agreed to accept independence as long as a yet-to-be-elected Congress was given the right to appoint a European nobleman as emperor. The Church, the country's largest landowner, backed the deal (Archer 2003, 304). Iturbide intended to build a state similar to the Brazilian Empire, although Brazil had a much shorter war of independence and counted with Dom Pedro I. If the monarchic project was somehow surprising but feasible in Brazil, it was a remote possibility in Mexico.

Iturbide's monarchy failed. The Mexican-born politicians formed the majority in Congress and vetoed the coronation of a foreign emperor. Spain did not accept Mexico's independence, which reduced the legitimacy of the Spaniards in the new state. Short of cash, the government forced Spanish traders to lend 1.3 million pesos, which deteriorated the little support Iturbide had among the elite in Mexico City. It did not take much for a military rebel to lead a revolution that deposed the ruler and established a republic in 1822. The rebel was General Anonio López de Santa Anna, the most prominent and controversial leader of Mexico's early post-colonial history (Llorens 2006, 36).

The end of the monarchy did not make politics less polarised. Traders and civil servants from the old Metropolis opposed Mexican-born landowners and local oligarchs. The former group defended a centralised state and the latter stood for federalism. Guadalupe Victoria (1824–1829), the first Mexican president, attempted to reach a compromise by combining monarchists and federalists in a single cabinet. Yet Spain's refusal to accept Mexico's sovereignty weakened the centralists and created opposition among federalists, who controlled Congress (Anna 2001).

A frustrated Spanish invasion triggered a monarchist uprising in 1827. Troops led by the half-native war veteran General Vicente Guerrero (1829–1830) defeated Spain. Guerrero ran for office in the following year but lost for Manuel Pedraza, who had the support of the monarchists. He contested the results and took office in a coup. The new president exiled many monarchists and, with troops under the command of Santa Anna, defeated a second Spanish invasion. The victory did not guarantee stability and Vice-President Anastacio Bustamante (1830–1832), a centralist connected to Iturbide, deposed Guerrero in 1830. Santa Anna took power for the first time in 1833 through another coup. He was subsequently deposed but would occupy the presidency again on ten other occasions (Archer 2003, 325–27).

In the 1830s, the centralists and federalists formed the Conservative and Liberal parties, which were going to polarise politics even more in the following four decades. The liberals defended a secular state and the nationalisation of the Church's vast lands, while the conservatives were clericals who counted with the support of the Church. While the Brazilian Conservative and Liberal parties shared a consensus over the monarchic state, the Mexican homonymous parties represented incompatible interests.

Santa Anna was independent from the political parties (Meyer et al. 2013, 324–28). Liberals controlled his first administration, which was targeted by a conservative revolt. Santa Anna managed to stay in power by forming a conservative cabinet. The new administration fought federalist and separatist rebels across the country. Santa Anna commanded and lost a campaign in Texas, then a remote Mexican state populated by native peoples and growing communities of US settlers. The separatists imprisoned the president and forced him to sign a treaty recognising the

Republic of Texas. A coup in Mexico deposed Santa Anna, who left to Cuba in exile (Archer 2003, 332).[1]

The Santa Anna administrations issued a series of "mandatory loans" against foreign merchants to finance the war in Texas. The traders claimed reparations and demanded protection from their respective governments, which launched foreign invasions that defined Mexico's mid-nineteenth-century history (Bazant 1968). France was particularly active in invading port cities—mainly Veracruz—to acquire compensations from customs. The first expedition happened in 1837, which provided Santa Anna with the opportunity to return to Mexico, fight the intruders and rehabilitate himself as a national hero. Santa Anna took office once again and waged war against the USA, which had by then incorporated Texas. The northern neighbour defeated the Mexican troops and conquered what are today the US states of California, Nuevo Mexico, Utah, Arizona and Colorado, which together with Texas corresponded to around half of Mexico's initial territory. The US Navy invaded Veracruz, forcing the government in Mexico City to accept that massive territorial loss.[2]

Santa Anna's last term, between 1853 and 1855, was his most autocratic. The dictatorship finished when Juan Álvarez, a leader from the Pacific coast, invaded Mexico City with his Army and deposed the old leader. Álvarez formed an influential liberal cabinet that counted with the Native Mexican descent Benito Juárez—to date a national hero—as the justice minister. The new administration issued anticlerical laws that included land expropriation, limitation of parish taxes and the end of ecclesiastical courts, which had managed civil affairs since colonial times (Fowler 2009, 289–315).

Financed by the Church, the Conservative Party took in arms against the liberal government, starting the Restoration War. The conservative General Félix María Zuloaga took Mexico City. The liberals fled to Veracruz, where Juárez created a parallel government. For three years, Mexico remained divided: The conservatives controlled the centre of the country and the liberals ruled the gulf coast and the north. The liberal government received support from the USA as an exchange for the free transit of troops during the American Civil War. Britain broke relations

[1] See Fowler (2009) for a study on Santa Anna.

[2] See Vázquez (2010) and Moreno (2013) for more on the US-Mexican war.

with the conservatives in 1860, when their government confiscated funds that British trades had deposited in their embassy. The international support helped the liberals to conquer Mexico City under the command of Juárez (Nzibo 1979, 161).

With the Treasury depleted, Juárez postponed payments to foreign traders who had been subject to forced loans. That act triggered a large-scale invasion. Britain, France and Spain formed a multinational military expedition to impose foreign control over customs collection in Veracruz (Zaragoza 1996, 92). The European fleets easily occupied the city in January 1862. Spain and Britain withdrew their troops four months later, but the French continued to battle until they took Mexico City. The invaders deposed Juárez and his cabinet left for the northern city of Chihuahua (Vázquez 2010). In an attempt to stretch the French Empire to the Americas, Napoleon III invited the Austrian noblemen Ferdinand Maximilian to be the emperor of Mexico. Most conservatives in Mexico City supported the new regime, in a re-edition of the 1820s project of a Mexican monarchy (Gille 1998, 446).

The liberals stood for the republican cause and received the decisive support of the US government once the Civil War was over. Republican forces made their way into Mexico City, while Napoleon III withdrew his troops from the country. An easy target, Maximilian was executed in 1866. The Conservative Party disappeared and Juárez was elected president. A more disciplined Army emerged from the war. It supported the new government and was less likely to intervene in politics. Mexico remained diplomatically isolated from Europe after the execution of Maximilian. Yet international relations stopped being a source of instability, for the disastrous French invasion made foreign powers less tempted to launch military expeditions in Mexico (Ridley 2001). The victory of Juárez' troops is still today celebrated as an achievement of the Mexican people in asserting their right for self-determination. Nationalism underpinned the formation of the state that appeared in the following decades.

The Serial Defaulter

Nueva España was home to the largest population and silver production in the Americas, but the war of independence destroyed mines, roads and the tax structure that existed in colonial Mexico. The conflict was costly, and the yet-to-be government borrowed extensively from domestic traders in a series of voluntary and forced loans. By the time Mexico became a sovereign state, its debt corresponded to over four times the first year's tax revenue (Ludlow and Marichal 1998).

As elsewhere in Latin America, the new government sought for foreign funds in London. Congress authorised the financial agent Francisco Migoni to negotiate a £1.6 million loan. Goldschmidt underwrote the operation in 1823 for £3.2 million, way above the previous stipulated value. The 5 per cent-type bonds were issued at a remarkably low 58% discount rate. The government agreed to the contract, which also stipulated that one-third of customs revenue would guarantee payments and that Migoni would receive the generous commission of 5% (Casasús 1880). The loan was a terrible deal for Mexico; the rest of Latin America borrowed at much better conditions. The deal was nevertheless profitable for the underwriters, for the bonds appeared on the secondary market at 70% of face value (Bazant 1968, 26–27).

Mexico borrowed again £3.2 million in 1825 from a London syndicate that included Richardson and Barclay, which had bought most of the 1823 loan. The new bonds were 6 per cent-type, but the discount rate and commission were more reasonable than before: 86.75% and 2%, respectively. Mexico serviced the debt up to 1827, when it joined the wave of Latin American defaults. That year's world trade crisis depressed customs collection in a context of fragile fiscal accounts. Also, Barclay went bust in 1826, and Mexico lost £450 thousand from the previous year's loan it had deposited in the bank (Ludlow and Marichal 1998).

External shocks may explain the timing of the default, but structurally unsound fiscal accounts conditioned the suspension of payments. The succession of coups, wars and invasions imposed a heavy toll on the Treasury, and the government ran rather large and persistent deficits. The figures are imprecise, but estimates indicate that expenditure was on average 88% higher than tax revenue from 1827 to 1862, when the French occupation began (INEGI 1990, 627).

The government borrowed domestically to finance the deficit. According to contemporary sources, the domestic debt stock increased from 30 million pesos in 1831 to 92.4 million pesos in 1848—the equivalent of 2.6 and shocking 11.7 times tax revenue, respectively.[3] Part of that borrowing consisted of arbitrary loans that the government imposed on foreign trades. As explained in the previous section, forced loans were

[3]Calculated from Payno (1862, 12–15) and INEGI (1990, 199–201).

the excuse for France, Britain and Spain to take the customs office of Veracruz, which deteriorated Mexico's fiscal accounts even further. Domestic credit was expensive—interest rates varied from 30% to up to 200% per year (Ludlow and Marichal 1998, 190). Creditors demanded a progressively larger share of customs revenue to secure payment on their debt. Santa Anna administration hypothecated 15% of all customs to service the debt in 1834, a rate that it subsequently increased to 32% in 1839. People such as Finance Minister Anastacio Bustamante, himself a public creditor, negotiated these deals on behalf of the state (Tenenbaum 1998, 67).

Mexico was on the silver standard, and thus the government could not print money to finance the deficit. New foreign loans stood as the most sustainable alternative to public finance. Yet the bondholders of the debt Mexico had issued in London in the 1820s imposed an embargo that financially isolated the country. The government tried to convert the so-called London debt into new bonds to clear its record abroad, but conditions were adverse and the government lacked funds to honour the conversion. High officials agreed on the issuing of new bonds every time they came to terms with the creditors, and the debt reached £15.6 million in 1858, which corresponded to almost twice that year's tax revenue.[4] The conversions also increased tax hypothecation, which reached nothing less than 49% of the customs revenue in Veracruz and 25% in the pacific ports (Montellano 1886, 27; Revueltas 2005, 69).

Unsurprisingly, the government never honoured the London debt. It only paid substantial sums at the end of the war with the USA, when Mexico received US$12 million in reparations from the American government. However, the bulk of that revenue financed domestic conflicts, and only US$2.5 million went to British bondholders (Tenenbaum 1998, 323; Bazant 1968, 51–66).

The French occupation of the 1860s briefly opened foreign markets to Mexico. Barings proposed to share the subscription of the first Mexican loan under Maximilian with the British banks Glyn Mills and Rothschilds, the latter of which sent an agent to Mexico City (Gille 1998, 131–32). Informed of Mexico's hopelessly unsound accounts,

[4]Calculated from Casasús (1896, 43, 141) and INEGI (1990, 627).

Rothschilds conditioned the loan on French guarantees (Revueltas 2005, 140). Napoleon III did not back the debt, and Barings and Rothschilds left Glyn Mills alone to underwrite the operation with the French bank Peréire Brothers. The Maximilian government borrowed £15.6 million at 6% interests and 63% discount in two loans issued in 1864 and 1865. The syndicate floated only £500,000 in London, the remaining of the bonds being issued in Paris under the name of *petit bleu* (Payno 1868).

The lending did not make fiscal accounts sound. Maximilian recognised the debt Mexico owned to French traders and agreed to pay 270 million francs in war reparations to France. In total, Mexico was to remit 66 million francs in a first allotment, followed by yearly instalments of 25 million francs (Payno 1862, 775–76). The new loans were entirely used to cover those expenses, and the old London debt remained on default. Meanwhile, republican troops led by Juárez marched towards Mexico City and deposed Maximilian (Gille 1998, 147). Once in office, Juárez repudiated the *petit bleu* as a symbol of foreign invasion. Repudiation did not involve the British debt, but the government lacked funds to service it and Mexico remained financially isolated in the following two decades (Bazant 1968, 86–87).

The Rise of Porfirio Díaz

The republican victory over Maximilian reshaped Mexico forever. The Conservative Party vanished altogether with the foreign ruler. Yet the country was still shaken by coups, battles and uprisings. Veterans of the country's many wars and the American Civil War formed bandit groups, the *bandoleros*, who assaulted travellers and towns across the country. Indigenous peoples revolted in the south, where they created a semi-independent state, and in the underpopulated north, where Apaches controlled vast territories (Vanderwood 1992). Political institutions were far from solid at the state level. The 1857 Constitution, the groundwork of the Liberal Party, prohibited re-elections, but Juárez ran for a second term in 1871. The president defeated the war hero General Porfirio Díaz, who contested the result. Díaz capitulated after a quick battle between his forces and the government's troops. Juárez died in the following year, and Sebastián Lerdo de Tejada (1872–1876) won an election organised after the president's death (Perry 1978, 154).

Tejada was an eminent liberal that participated in the 1857 cabinet and fought the French occupation. His administration was the most stable and effective the country had so far. Tejada created the Senate, reducing the power of the relatively more volatile Lower Chamber. His forces gained battles over separatists and rebel local leaders. Tejada ran for office 1876 and, once again, Díaz contested his candidacy for re-election. This time Díaz did not participate in the pulling; instead, he took in arms to depose Tejada. The future dictator took office in what turned out to be Mexico's last coup of the nineteenth century.

It is ironic that the long period of peace and stability known as the Porfiriato started with a violent incident, in which the future dictator fought to prevent a re-election. Nevertheless, the Porfirian regime was different from the repressive administrations of previous dictators, such as Santa Anna. It promoted long-term changes that delivered economic growth and improved state capacity. Díaz did not convert himself into the well-known dictator right after the 1876 coup. His first administration respected the opposition and the press. What is more, he stepped down and did not run for re-election at the end of that presidency in 1879 (Rosenzweig 2005).

Díaz privatised communal land, from which landowners profited a great deal. The reform helped the central government to cut deals with local elites. The losers were the indigenous communities whose access to land had been protected by law since colonial times. Land privatisation created an elastic labour supply that contributed to economic growth but increased inequality. As will be studied in Chapter 8, land reform was the main reason why insurgents raised against the dictator in the 1910 Revolution.

The Army grew stronger and more disciplined as Díaz created military academies and imported modern war machinery. The government also created militias known as the *rurales*. Besides balancing the power of the Army and local authorities in national politics, the *rurales* also reduced the activities of the *bandolero* groups by fighting as well as incorporating their members (Vanderwood 1992). After half a century, the state was finally imposing the monopoly of violence over the country. Díaz reached a compromise with the Church. The president preserved the anticlerical reforms put forward in the 1857 Constitution but did not repress dioceses that accumulated wealth. Finally, Mexico re-established diplomatic relations with France and Spain, and the government started to work towards a deal with Britain. Díaz intended to strengthen relations with Europe to balance the growing economic influence of the USA, which he and his officials saw as a major threat to Mexico's sovereignty (Weiner 2000, 668).

Minister Manuel González (1880–1884) won the 1879 election with Díaz's blessing. Contemporaries considered his administration inept and corrupt and blamed the president for the fiscal crisis that hit the country in the mid-1880s, which I will detail in the next section. Díaz easily won the 1884 election, which marks the beginning of his quarter-century-long government, during which the president built his autocratic regime. The dictator abolished political parties, reduced the role of Congress to rubble-stamping presidential decrees and appointed governors and judges across the country (Anna 2001, 102).

Railways, Banamex and Fiscal Accounts

Fiscal account remained unsound after the fall of Maximilian. Foreign creditors imposed a new embargo on Mexico following the 1864 moratorium, and the government borrowed domestically at expensive rates. Table 6.1 reports fiscal data. It compares the figures the government published in *Cuentas del Tesoro Federal* and the reconstructed series published in *Estadísticas Históricas de México* (INEGI 1990). The series differ greatly, but both sources show recurrent deficits. The modern data is more accurate, especially for the earlier period.

Customs responded on average to 57% of tax collection in the period covered in Table 6.1. Mexico ran a merchandise trade deficit: Excluding precious metals, exports were about half of imposts (Ficker 2002, 249–50). The deficit was roughly equal to silver exports, which in macroeconomic terms consisted in monetary outflow—Mexico was on the silver standard. Adding merchandise and precious metals together, Mexican exports per capita were the lowest in Latin America in the 1860s—US$2.3 per year against a continental average of US$8.9 (Bulmer-Thomas 2014, 69). Without an increase in merchandise exports, the amount of silver the country could remit determined its

Table 6.1 Mexico's fiscal data, 1869–1888 (million Mexican pesos) (*Source Cuentas del Tesoro Federal*; INEGI (1990, 627))

Year	*Cuentas del Tesoro*		*Estadísticas Historicas de México*	
	Revenue	*Expenditure*	*Revenue*	*Expenditure*
1869–1870	16.69	16.69	14.50	18.30
1870–1871	18.89	18.89	14.50	20.80
1871–1872	20.35	20.35	20.60	21.10
1872–1873	21.51	21.51	21.20	22.90
1873–1874	17.90	22.35	21.70	23.90
1874–1875	17.60	22.93	21.00	24.10
1875–1876	17.27	22.64	16.50	24.80
1876–1877	14.39	18.18	16.50	25.80
1877–1878	19.77	30.35	16.10	19.00
1878–1879	17.81	30.08	17.80	21.70
1879–1880	21.12	22.18	17.80	18.80
1880–1881	23.17	25.32	19.44	23.10
1881–1882	28.28	37.38	21.08	25.20
1882–1883	30.69	45.37	22.72	27.00
1883–1884	28.29	50.82	24.36	30.70
1884–1885	27.23	51.91	26.00	25.80
1885–1886	26.77	31.67	28.00	38.90
1886–1887	31.30	38.78	29.00	33.30
1887–1888	33.87	56.84	32.00	36.20

capacity to import. When remittances were too intense, however, falling means of payments reduced credit domestically, which had negative fiscal impacts. In short, Mexico needed to boost non-silver exports to run sound fiscal accounts.

The lack of a railway system limited domestic trade and merchandise exports. Large mountain ranges across vast dry territories kept transports costs high and the countryside isolated from the coast. Railways were also politically important. New lines would increase land value and speed up the deployment of troops, contributing to the co-optation and submission of local leaders. The Tejada administration attracted foreign investment to build the first railway, which linked Mexico City to VeraCruz. That was too little too late: Countries like Brazil and Argentina had started to develop railway systems two decades earlier (Coatsworth 1981, 97–103). The building of lines was fiscally expensive, for the companies demanded generous subsidies and profit guarantees

Table 6.2 Cost of railways and the domestic debt in Mexico, 1881–1887 (*Source Cuentas del Tesoro Federal*)

	Railways (i)		*Domestic debt (ii)*		*Total (i + ii)*	
	(% tax revenue)	*(% expenditure)*	*(% tax revenue)*	*(% expenditure)*	*(% tax revenue)*	*(% expenditure)*
1881–1882	28.46	21.53	23.23	17.57	51.69	39.10
1882–1883	40.15	27.16	17.26	11.68	57.41	38.84
1883–1884	21.56	12.00	60.18	33.49	81.74	45.49
1884–1885	42.70	22.40	41.57	21.80	84.27	44.20
1885–1886	3.58	3.03	14.17	11.98	17.76	15.01
1886–1887	10.81	8.72	13.85	11.18	24.66	19.90
1887–1888	5.70	3.40	52.44	31.25	58.14	34.65

(Riguzzi 1995, 165). Díaz first administration subsidised the construction of railways, but it was under González that the promotion of new projects peaked. The system grew six times during his presidency, reaching 6,000 km in 1885. Yet the costs of such programme were enormous: Table 6.2 shows that railways consumed a great share of the budget.

Mexico faced a fiscal dilemma: The government needed to subsidise the building of railways to increase foreign trade and raise customs revenue in the long run, but the subsidies were so costly that railways deteriorated fiscal accounts in the short term. The official data reported in Table 6.1 show that expenditure was almost two times higher than revenue in the last two years of González administration. The fiscal crisis also appears in the reconstructed data, although less intensively. The accounts were unsound because of a short-sighted solution to the fiscal dilemma: The government borrowed unsustainably from semi-official banks. The first of these banks was the Nacional Mexicano, which the Paris-based financier Edouard Noetzlin and Mexican investors funded in 1882. Noetzlin would become a central figure in Mexico's finance. The Nacional was an internationalised enterprise: European investors held over 60% of its stocks. The list included the French banks Banque Franco-Egyptienne and Société Générade de Crédit Industrielle et Commerciale, the London-based financier Cassel, the Dutch financier Lipmann, the German banker Gerson von Bleichroeder and Noetzlin himself. That was a way the government and foreign creditors found to bypass the financial embargo on Mexico (Ludlow 1990, 982).

The Nacional Mexicano was closely related to the government: It held a thirty-year-long monopoly on monetary emission and the administration of fiscal accounts, including the collection of taxes. In other words, the government handed its books to the bank, which, in return, financed the fiscal deficit. That reduced the government's autonomy over payments, compensating for the high risk of default. González administration over-borrowed, raising the cost of servicing the domestic debt. To make matters worse, poor harvests depressed taxation and a fall in silver prices limited Mexico's capacity to import, decreasing customs revenue. The services on the debt reached 60% of tax revenue in 1883–1884, as shown in Table 6.2.

The government demanded a level of credit that the Nacional Mexicano could not provide, resulting in a run on that bank (Marichal 1993, 422). Noetzlin went to Mexico to arrange a solution with President González. They agreed to merge the Nacional Mexicano with the Banco Mercantil Mexicano, a discount bank owned by local traders (Ludlow 1990, 1106). The operation created the Banco Nacional de México (Banamex) in 1884. Banamex held the same prerogatives of Nacional Mexicano, but its larger size enabled more lending (Maurer 2002, 22). As a result, the domestic public debt increased 2.6 times from 1884 to 1888 (Maurer 2002, 22).

The government forcibly converted more expensive short-term debt into consolidated 5% bonds (Ludlow and Marichal 1998, 196). Together with a recovered taxation following the mid 1880s economic crisis, the conversion reduced the ratio between services and tax revenue under Díaz. The new president also suspended most railway subsidies, which together with the costs of servicing the debt declined from 84% to 18% of tax collection, as appears in Table 6.2.

The forced conversion and subsidy cuts did not cause political instability nor did it compromise economic development, in a flagrant contrast with the abrupt policy changes of the past. Instead of penalising the new administration, Banamex intensified its business with the government after Díaz took office. Moreover, the bulk of the railway project launched under González was close to completion, finally reducing Mexico's lack of logistic infrastructure. Political stability, state capacity and a growing railway sector created the conditions for the government to solve Mexico's persistent fiscal problem. However, Mexico was still under a financial embargo, which would only end after a settlement on the London debt.

Díaz, Noetzlin and Sovereign Debt

A question arises from the role of Banamex in helping the government to deal with the mid-1880s fiscal crisis: What did its manager Noetlizn gain from it? Maurer (2002, 93–114) and Passananti (2007) stress the importance of the privileges the government handed to the bank. As an exchange for financing unsound fiscal accounts, the government handed sources of rent such as monetary printing and government banking to Banamex. Without disputing this claim, I argue that Noetzlin also intended to gain from Mexico' eventual return to the international financial market. The managing of the sovereign debt crucially defined Noetzlin's decision of doing banking with the Mexican government. Evidence suggests that the underwriting of sovereign loans in Europe rather than the issuing of domestic debt in Mexico was the final goal behind the creation of Banamex.

Shortly after founding Banamex, Noetzlin agreed with President González that he would negotiate a settlement on the British debt on behalf of the Mexican government. The financier would also organise a syndicate to underwrite a new loan in Europe, with which the government would redeem the debt issued in the settlement. The contract included a flagrant conflict of interests, for it established that "Mr. Noetzlin will arrange with the Bank [Banamex] the commission he is entitled to receive for the service."[5] Banamex established the commission at 13 million pesos, 10 million of which (the equivalent of £1.76 million) the bank would pay to Noetzlin alone (Ludlow and Marichal 1998, 16–17). The financier drafted a contract with the Committee of Mexican Bondholders, but González failed to pass the deal in Congress. Mexico arranged a new settlement in the following year. This time the Finance Minister Manuel Dublán—a Mexican national rather than a foreign agent—negotiated the deal on behalf of the state, which unsurprisingly included lower costs (Marichal 1993, 363).

Congress frustrated Noetzlin's plans a few months before Porfirio Díaz replaced González in office. A weak president about to leave public life, González had little bargaining power to negotiate with foreign

[5] *AHB* box 2, folder 26.

agents. That was not the case of Díaz, who won the 1884 election by a landslide (Salvucci 2013, 284–85). By excluding Noetzlin from the settlement, the new president reduced the rent the financiers intended to acquire from Mexico.[6] Yet the government did not become entirely hostile to the financier, who organised the issuing of a new loan, as had been agreed in the contract signed in 1884. The syndicate that underwrote the 1888 loan included some of Noetzlin's closest associates: Banque Franco-Egyptian, Lipman and Bleichroeder (Mexico 1925, 311–13). All these underwriters held shares of Banamex, which also participated in the operation.[7]

Mexico Returns to the Market

It is striking that Mexico borrowed abroad through Noetzlin's syndicate four years after Congress aborted the debt conversion that he had negotiated with the Committee of Mexican Bondholders. This is particularly intriguing because the conditions of the loan were far from attractive. Mexico issued the 1888 bonds at 78.50% of par, and the underwriters sold them at a 16.38% margin. The operation was for £10.5 million, and thus the banks profited £1.72 million with the sale of the bonds—almost the amount Mexico would have paid Noetzlin had he converted the British debt in 1884.[8]

Before the government signed the 1888 loan contract, the bad borrowing conditions it was about to accept were the subject of revealing correspondence between Díaz and Francisco Mena, who represented the Finance Ministry in Europe and considered Noetzlin "very dangerous to our country."[9] Mena understood that the issuing price was too low and the commission, at first established at 2.50%, was too high.[10] The

[6]Passananti (2007, 105) also found evidence that Díaz intended to limit Noetzlin's gains, although he focuses on the activities of Banamex in Mexico rather than the management of the sovereign debt.

[7]Ludlow (1990, 982–84).

[8]Mexico (1925).

[9]*AGPD* Mena to Díaz, 17 July 1888, box 23, no. 7561.

[10]*AGPD* Mena to Díaz, 26 January 1888, box 23, no. 3164.

syndicate reduced the commission to 1.25%, but the issuing discount remained unchanged. Díaz explained the need to go ahead with the operation in the following way:

> I owe millions of pesos to the National Bank [Banamex], which has got half of the Federal Treasury in its pocket, but nonetheless keeps on providing me with funds [...] because [Banamex] has its sights on the [1888] loan, for which it will demand to be my confidant with Bleichroeder.[11]

The government (which Díaz referred to as himself) depended on Banamex to finance the domestic debt, which totalled £22.8 million in 1887–1888.[12] The quote suggests that Banamex continued to finance such an unsound borrower because Noetzlin aimed to organise the first sovereign loan of the Porfiriato. Maintaining a line of credit to the government gave the financier considerable leverage over Díaz, who feared that Banamex would retaliate by suspending the state's access to domestic-denominated credit if Noetzlin was not allowed to arrange the foreign-denominated loan. The literature on Banamex highlights that the founders of the bank created it to acquire rents domestically (Maurer 2002; Passananti 2007). It is evident from the quote above that Noetzlin and his partners also intended to use Banamex to extract rents from the sovereign debt.

Another reason that explains why Díaz accepted the 1888 loan was the urgent need of credit to honour the agreement signed with the Committee of Mexican Bondholders in 1885. The settlement consolidated the old debt at £15 million and established that the government could buy back the conversion bonds at a 40% discount before December 1890. Even with such a deduction, the obligations amounted the equivalent of 34.5% of the taxes collected from 1888–1889 to 1890–1891.[13] These figures led Díaz to declare that "the situation is very distressing above all because we are portraying a state of well-being that does not exist."[14] Shortly later, he informed Mena that "we have a bit more than two years to avoid a noisy scandal that would ruin the credit

[11] *AGDP* Díaz to Mena, 26 January 1888, box 23, no. 3165.

[12] *Cuentas del Tesoro Federal.*

[13] Calculated from Mexico (1925), and INEGI (1990, 627).

[14] *AGPD* Díaz to Mena, 26 January 1888, box 23, no. 3165.

that with so much difficulty we are now able to raise."[15] Mexico needed new credit to prevent the imposition of a new financial embargo. For this reason, the government not only accepted to issue the new loan at a low discount; it also included in the lending contract that the borrowing resources were to finance the redemption of the bonds issued in the 1885 conversion, and the remainder was to service the domestic debt held by Banamex (Mexico 1925).

Díaz Refuses a Patron Bank

Noeztlin's syndicate underwrote the 1888 loan in spite of Mexico's precarious fiscal accounts. As explained above, the lending was profitable to the underwriters. A long-term factor also explains why the bankers agreed upon the operation. Market conditions were favourable in the late 1880s, and the underwriters had reasons to anticipate substantial profits from future loans.[16] The 1888 loan financed the 1885 settlement, clearing Mexico's record and conclusively opening its access to foreign markets. The redemption of the old British debt generated opportunities for the underwriters of the Mexican debt.

Since Mexico was not on the market before 1888, it is not possible to assess the improvement in Mexican credit before and after that year's loan. Yet press reports suggest that the redemption of the conversion bonds was a watershed in terms of reputation. The coverage was rather negative during most of the 1880s. Early in that decade, *The Investor's Monthly Manual* published that "the Mexican Government was known to have committed themselves very heavily in the direction of railway subsidies (which) had crippled revenue a good deal."[17] By the time of the 1885 conversion, *The Times* published that "resources do not exist to meet new and acknowledged obligations."[18] *The Economist* advised that "bondholders (…) would do well not to be too sanguine to the ability of Mexico to redeem the promises she is now making."[19]

[15] *AGPD* Díaz to Mena, 21 March 1888, box 23, no. 3199.

[16] Salvucci (2013, 287) also reaches this conclusion.

[17] *Investor's Monthly Manual*, 1883, vol. 8, p. 247.

[18] *The Times*, 30 June 1885, issue 31486, p. 9.

[19] *The Economist*, 5 September 1885, issue 2193, p. 1083.

All that changed in 1889, when the *Economist* published that political stability enabled "a reduction of the military force" from which "a saving of a million dollars will be realised."[20] In the following years, the newspaper printed that "thanks to a continuance of tranquillity (...) the revenue of Mexico has for a long time been enjoying steady expansion."[21] Similarly, *The Times* highlighted that "the relations between Mexico and the rest of the world have undergone a radical change" and that the "peace which has prevailed has rendered these reforms possible."[22]

Noetzlin and his associates intended to continue profiting from Mexico's sovereign debt. Already in 1888, he informed Díaz that "the group that made the [1888] loan wishes to participate in the finance of the Tehuantepec railway," a state-owned line then under construction.[23] Mexico borrowed abroad to finance the Tehuantepec in 1889, but it did so through a different syndicate composed by Dresdner and Seligman. The new loan was for £2.7 million. Commission was 1.5%, higher than the 1% charged in the previous operation, but interest rate was 5% rather than 6%. Discount rate was 77.5%, resulting in a 3.53% risk premium, substantially lower than the 4.85% applied to the 1888 loan. The revenue from Tehuantepec guaranteed services, which explains why the loan was cheaper. Yet Dresdner and Seligman profited significantly less than the underwriters of the 1888 loan—the price run-up between issuing and floating was more reasonable at 6.13%.

Noeztlin and Bleichroeder would have consolidated their influence over Mexican finance had they underwritten the second loan of the Porfiriato. That did not happen as the Díaz administration revealed its preference for the diversification of credit sources without a patron bank. However, the Mexicans did not suspend relations with Bleichroeder, which underwrote a new loan in 1890. Besides Banamex, the British bank Gibbs also participated in the operation. Conditions were significantly better than in 1888: 93.5% rather than the previous 78.5%

[20] *The Economist*, 27 April 1889, issue 2383, p. 687.

[21] *The Economist* issue, 8 February 1890, issue 2424, p. 170.

[22] *The Times*, 21 September 1889, issue 32810, p. 3.

[23] *AGPD* Noetzlin to Díaz, 18 April 1888, box 23, no. 3820.

discount. As will be explained in the next chapter, the underwriters lost substantially with the operation because falling silver prices and the Baring Crisis reduced the quotation of Mexican bonds.

A newcomer to the global market, Bleichroeder continued underwriting Mexican loans even though Díaz frustrated his pretention of becoming the country's patron bank. Bleichroeder depended on the government to become an important underwriter, for Mexico was the bank's opening door to the global market. To some extent, the same applied to Noetzlin. By 1890, these two financiers did not count with the power over the government they have had in 1888. Mexico's return to the market empowered the government, allowing it to borrow at better conditions from different banks. Yet that was little in comparison with what the Mexican negotiations were going to do in the following decade. Chapter 7 will show how the government changed the balance of power vis-à-vis the underwriters of its debt in the late 1890s and the 1900s.

Conclusion

Noetzlin and the 1888 syndicate had the upper hand over Mexico in the 1880s because of the government's terrible payment record and unsound fiscal accounts. Díaz had to accept the poor conditions the financiers offered. However, the president refused to grant a monopoly on the country's debt. The underwriters had an undistinguishable position in the world market, which was consistent with Mexico's record. Premier banks would not underwrite the debt of a serial defaulter. That limited the government's incentives to agree on patron banking. By the early 1890s, Mexico had redeemed its old debt, therefore clearing its name. A better reputation placed high officials in a stronger position to negotiate new loans, beginning an approach to sovereign debt that persisted for the rest of the Porfiriato.

References

Archival Sources

AGPD Archivo General Porfirio Díaz.
Correndencias.

AHB Archivo Histórico Banamex.
Contrato para el arreglo de la deuda mexicana en Londres.

Official and Contemporary Sources

Casasús, Joaquín D. 1880. *Historia de la deuda contraída en Londres, con un apéndice sobre el estado actual de la Hacienda Pública*. Mexico City: Imprenta del Gobierno.

———. 1896. *Estudios monetarios: La cuestión de la plata en México; el problema monetario, la depreciación de la plata y sus remedios, historia de los impuestos sobre el oro y la plata*. Mexico City: Oficina impresora del timbre.

INEGI. 1990. *Estadísticas históricas de México*. Mexico City: Instituto Nacional de Estadística, Geografía e Informática.

Mexico. 1925. *Colección de leyes y disposiciones relacionadas con la deuda exterior de México*. Mexico City: Secretaría de Hacienda y Crédito Público.

———. *Cuentas de Tesoro Federal formada por la Tesorería General de la Federación*. Mexico City: Tipografía de la Oficina Impresora del Timbre.

Payno, Manuel. 1862. *Mexico and Her Financial Questions with England, Spain and France: Report by Order of the Supreme Constitutional Government of the Mexican Republic*. Mexico City: I. Cumplido.

———. 1868. *Cuentas, gastos, aceedores y otros asuntos del tiempo de la intervencion francesa y del Imperio*. Mexico City: I. Cumplido.

The Economist.

The Investor's Monthly Manual.

The Times.

Secondary Sources

Anna, Timothy E. 2001. *Forging Mexico, 1821–1835*. Lincoln: University of Nebraska Press.

Archer, Christon I. 2003. *The Birth of Modern Mexico, 1780–1824*. Lanham: Rowman & Littlefield Publishers.

Bazant, Juan. 1968. *Historia de la deuda exterior de México, 1823–1946*. Mexico City: El Colegio de México.

Bulmer-Thomas, Victor. 2014. *The Economic History of Latin America since Independence*. Cambridge: Cambridge University Press.

Coatsworth, John H. 1981. *Growth Against Development: The Economic Impact of Railroads in Porfirian Mexico*. DeKalb: Northern Illinois University Press.

Ficker, Sandra K. 2002. "Nuevas Series Del Comercio Exterior de México, 1870–1929." *Revista de Historia Económica* 20 (02):213–70.

Fowler, Will. 2009. *Santa Anna of Mexico*. Lincoln: University of Nebraska Press.

Gille, Geneviève. 1998. "Los capitales franceses y la expedición a México." In *Un siglo de deuda pública en México*, edited by Leonor Ludlow and Carlos Marichal, 125–51. Mexico City: Instituto Mora.

Llorens, Antònia P. 2006. *La deuda española en México: diplomacia y política en torno a un problema financiero, 1821–1890*. Mexico City: Colegio de México.
Ludlow, Leonor. 1990. "El Banco Nacional Mexicano y el Banco Mercantil Mexicano: radiografía social de sus primeros accionistas, 1881–1882." *Historia Mexicana* 39 (4):979–1027.
Ludlow, Leonor, and Carlos Marichal. 1998. "La deuda pública en México en el siglo XIX: el dificil tránsito hacia la modernidad." In *Un siglo de deuda pública en México*, edited by Ludlow, Leonor and Marichal, Carlos, 7–24. Mexico City: Instituto Mora.
Marichal, Carlos. 1993. "El Manejo de la Deuda Pública y la Crisis Financiera de 1884–1885." In *Los negocios y las ganancias de la colonia al México moderno*, edited by Leonor Ludlow and Jorge S. Riquer, 421–46. Mexico City: Instituto Mora.
Maurer, Noel. 2002. *The Power and the Money: The Mexican Financial System, 1876–1932*. Stanford: Stanford University Press.
Meyer, Michael C., William L. Sherman, and Susan M. Deeds. 2013. *The Course of Mexican History*. Oxford: Oxford University Press.
Montellano, Mariano O. 1886. *Apuntes para la liquidación de la deuda contraida en Londres*. Mexico City: Imprenta del Gobierno Federal en Palacio.
Moreno, Francisco M. 2013. *México mutilado: la raza maldita*. Mexico City: Grupo Planeta.
Nzibo, Abdulrahman. 1979. "Relations between Great Britain and Mexico, 1820–1880." PhD dissertation, Glasgow: University of Glasgow.
Passananti, Thomas P. 2007. ""Nada de Papeluchos!" Managing Globalization in Early Porfirian Mexico." *Latin American Research Review* 42 (3):101–28.
Perry, Laurens B. 1978. *Juárez and Díaz: Machine Politics in Mexico*. DeKalb: Northern Illinois University Press.
Revueltas, Silvestre V. 2005. *Deuda y diplomacia: la relación México-Gran Bretana, 1824–1884*. Mexico City: UNAM.
Ridley, Jasper. 2001. *Maximilian and Juarez*. New Haven: Phoenix.
Riguzzi, Paolo. 1995. "Inversión extranjera e interés nacional en los ferrocarriles mexicanos, 1880–1914." In *Las inversiones extranjeras en América Latina, 1850–1930: nuevos debates y problemas en historia ecónmica comparada*, edited by Carlos Marichal, 347–68. Mexico City: El Colegio de México.
Rosenzweig, Fernando. 2005. "El desarrollo económico de México de 1877 a 1911." In *Historia económica de México*, edited by Enrique Cárdenas, 43–67. Mexico City: Fondo de Cultura Económica.
Salvucci, Richard J. 2013. *Politics, Markets, and Mexico's "London Debt", 1823–1887*. Cambridge: Cambridge University Press.
Tenenbaum, Barbara A. 1998. "El mercado monetario y la deuda interna de México, 1821–1855." In *La moneda en México, 1750–1920*, edited by José A. Vázquez and José E. Covarrubias, 52–74. Mexico City: El Colegio de México.

Vanderwood, Paul J. 1992. *Disorder and Progress: Bandits, Police, and Mexican Development*. Lanham: Rowman & Littlefield.

Vázquez, Josefina Zoraida. 2010. "War and Peace with the United States." In *The Oxford History of Mexico*, edited by William Beezley and Michael Meyer, 319–48. Oxford University Press.

Weiner, Richard. 2000. "Battle for Survival: Porfirian Views of the International Marketplace." *Journal of Latin American Studies* 32 (3):645–70.

Weller, Leonardo. 2015. "Government versus Bankers: Sovereign Debt Negotiations in Porfirian Mexico, 1888–1910." *Journal of Economic History* 75 (4):1030–57.

Zaragoza, José. 1996. *Historia de la deuda externa de México, 1823–1861*. Mexico City: UNAM.

CHAPTER 7

The Bankers' Beloved Dictatorship: Mexico, 1890–1910

Mexico established a reputation as a borrower in the 1890s, a decade that started with a crisis. Falling silver prices reduced exports, depressed tax revenue and depreciated the exchange rate. The government nearly defaulted on the debt, and Bleichroeder, its major underwriter, granted a rescue loan. The crisis forced policymakers to reduce expenditure and increase taxation, which resulted in sound fiscal accounts when silver prices stabilised in the mid-1890s. Mexican risk fell consistently until the end of the Porfiriato in 1911. Yet the government borrowed three times in 1899, 1904 and 1910 below the market rate. This is a financial paradox, for seniority implies that new debt should pay more than older obligations to attract bondholders.

The 1899 and 1910 loans were conversion operations launched when the market was trading the older debt around par, which constituted an upper price limit as the government was about to redeem it at that level. Hence, it was reasonable to anticipate a fall in Mexican risk once the new bonds were floated at lower interest rates. However, this chapter shows that these conversion loans would not have been so cheap had the Mexican negotiators not pressured for better terms. The 1904 loan had no apparent reason for being floated below the market rate, as it was not a conversion operation nor did it involve special guarantees. The underwriters intended to issue those bonds above Mexican risk until the final proposal, which they offered after two years of negotiations.

Díaz government was collecting the gains from an improved reputation combined with the choice of not having a patron bank. Reputation

L. Weller, *Sovereign Debt Crises and Negotiations in Brazil and Mexico, 1888-1914*, https://doi.org/10.1007/978-3-319-73633-4_7

raised the government's power over the banks and enabled Mexico's negotiators to bargain with different underwriters, forcing them to agree upon surprisingly good borrowing terms.

The Establishment of a Reputation

Silver prices fell sharply in the early 1890s, causing a payment crisis in Mexico. The country depended on silver exports to finance a persistent merchandise trade deficit (excluding precious metals). Imports fell by over a third, which must have depressed customs revenue. The government did not publish fiscal data during those four years, most probably as a deliberate measure to avoid revealing how unsound its accounts were (Rosales 1996, 113). The peso was pegged to silver, and the exchange rate depreciated by 59% between 1890 and 1894, raising the cost of servicing the newly issued foreign-denominated sovereign debt (INEGI 1990). What is more, the Baring Crisis reduced the flow of capital to Latin America as a whole (Mitchener and Weidenmier 2007). As a consequence, Mexican risk increased from about 3.5% at the beginning of the crisis in 1890 to a record high of 8% in 1893.[1]

The government would have probably defaulted had it not borrowed from Bleichroeder in 1893. The bank offered a loan for £3 million, 59% of which financed obligations on the sovereign debt and 10% went to Banamex.[2] Bleichroeder launched that operation in association with the British house Glyn Mills, whose involvement Cassel, a London-based financier, intermediated.[3] Bleichroeder required a twofold increase in the guarantees on the debt issued in 1888 and 1890 to launch the 1893 loan. The banker, who died that same year, feared that the 20% and 14% customs hypothecation stipulated in these loans' respective contracts would not cover the services on the debt. The government accepted the demand, which shows that the crisis had reduced its leverage over its principal underwriter.[4]

[1] See Fig. 1.2.

[2] Mexico (1925).

[3] *BC* Cassel to Beichroeder, 1 December 1893, Jewish Affairs folder, carton 33.6.

[4] *BC* Bleichroeder to Banamex, 29 August 1893, and Limantour to Bleichroder, 5 December 1893, Mexican 1893 Loan folder, carton 1. That state of affairs contrasts with the arrangement that led to the 1890 loan, as studied in Chapter 6.

The 1893 loan was issued at a 68% discount, lower than any other Mexican loan since the end of the financial embargo in 1888. Yet market conditions were worse than in the previous years, and the risk premium applied to the lending was 8% below Mexican risk, which characterises it as a rescue loan. Mexico would have jeopardised Bleichroeder internationalisation project had it defaulted on its debt, which created incentives for the granting of credit while silver prices were falling. The bonds only appeared on the market in 1895 at 73.8% of face value, which suggests that the underwriter held the debt until the price of Mexican securities recovered.[5]

Bleichroeder had reasons to expect that the debt crisis would be over once silver prices stabilised, for the government was implementing measures to improve fiscal accounts. I have not found evidence that the banker issued the loan for that reason, but it is reasonable to assume that he counted on the probability of profit from a price run-up when rescuing Mexico. The 1893 loan was a case of a rescue loan that not only protected the underwriter's reputation but also created profit opportunities—although it also involved risk apart from the cost of holding the bonds for two years.

Trade boomed once silver prices stabilised at low levels in the second half of the 1890s. Tax collection increased, fiscal accounts improved and Mexico finally established a reputation as a good borrower. The *Economist* (26 March 1898, p. 407) reported that "the position attained by Mexican Government finance in recent years [...] is a very creditable one, especially considering that it has been reached in face of considerable and unavoidable difficulties." Mexican risk fell rapidly, going from 8% to 4% between 1894 and 1895. It then reached 2% in the early 1900s and 1.5% in 1910.[6] That rate was not far above the level at which countries with no history of default and association with premier banks (such as Brazil) borrowed in London.

According to Tomz (2012), bad borrowers upgrade their status when they honour obligations in spite of adverse shocks—an argument discussed in Chapter 2. That was the case of Mexico during the silver crisis. Yet this is only one side of the story, for Bleichroeder's rescue loan helped the government to service the debt until silver prices stabilised, maintaining its record clean during bad times. Besides the commitment to debt contract, it also took cheap credit to make Mexico a creditworthy borrower.

[5] From *The Investor's Monthly Manual.*

[6] Calculated from Mexico (1925) and *The Investor's Monthly Manual.* See Fig. 1.2.

Table 7.1 Mexico's financial data, 1890–1909 (*Source* Cuentas del Tesoro Federal for official fiscal data; INEGI (1990, 627) for reconstructed fiscal data and exchange rate; Ficker (2002) for trade; Memoria de Hacienda for debt)

	Fiscal balance (% tax revenue)		*Merchandise*		*Debt service*		*Exchange rate (MX$/£) (1890 = 100)*
	Official	*Reconstructed*	*Exports (£ million)*	*Imports (£ million)*	*(% tax revenue)*	*(% exports)*	
1890–1891	−71.36	−1.05	7.15	9.98	0.95	0.83	100.50
1891–1892	–	–	7.48	9.01	–	–	111.52
1892–1893	–	–	8.78	8.93	–	–	123.51
1893–1894	–	–	7.86	6.25	–	7.80	149.20
1894–1895	5.86	−6.05	7.18	7.05	14.67	9.54	159.24
1895–1896	10.79	–	8.52	8.76	25.61	16.93	151.92
1896–1897	6.16	−0.21	9.44	8.76	26.95	15.39	160.94
1897–1898	1.68	–9.68	9.26	8.87	28.81	15.24	180.91
1898–1899	11.04	−1.92	10.14	10.43	24.12	13.78	174.59
1899–1900	9.26	−1.82	11.81	12.72	24.86	13.51	168.76
1900–1901	1.25	−1.37	11.59	13.46	20.86	11.21	170.49
1901–1902	4.63	0.80	12.85	13.46	20.08	9.48	184.06
1902–1903	4.10	7.14	13.51	15.59	21.49	10.46	195.10
1903–1904	3.42	6.25	14.97	16.16	19.37	10.56	178.36
1904–1905	−17.25	4.71	17.13	17.86	17.62	9.74	163.80
1905–1906	4.86	4.44	21.44	18.60	17.79	8.42	163.51
1906–1907	12.32	4.21	22.35	22.85	15.98	8.42	162.82
1907–1908	6.17	6.10	21.75	22.27	16.52	8.70	163.97
1908–1909	−5.70	−0.68	21.48	16.10	18.45	8.70	164.97
1909–1910	−1.06	0.00	23.90	19.96	17.29	7.89	164.20

Table 7.1 shows how merchandise exports increased rapidly and the government started running a fiscal surplus by the turn of the century. The official series is probably over-optimistic, but the reconstructed data also show that accounts improved. That was a novelty for Mexico, which had consistently ran deficits for most of the nineteenth century, as explained in Chapter 6.

Cheap silver partly explains the improvement in Mexico's fiscal accounts. The exchange rate depreciation had limited inflationary effects because the sale of indigenous land had broken up native communities, making the labour supply elastic (Rosenzweig 2005, 64; Catão 1998, 59). The *peso* depreciated in real terms during the silver crisis, and exports increased threefolds in the following ten years. Customs revenue grew on average by 11% per year between 1894 and 1910. While the tax base expanded, the government introduced new domestic duties, mainly on consumption goods, and prevented expenditure from rising as much as revenue (Carmagnani 1994, 146–56). The ratio between services and tax receipts fell both because of the increase in taxation and the adoption of the Gold Standard in 1904–1905, which stopped the secular depreciation of silver from weakening the *peso* (Sotelo and Eugenia 2009).

The implementation of orthodox fiscal policy relates to the rise of the *científicos*, a group of policymakers who considered sound budgets a precondition for the building of state capacity. The reduction of borrowing costs—this chapter's topic—was a means towards that end. The *científicos* aimed to attract foreign capital to promote economic growth and increase taxation, with the final goal of making the state strong enough to protect national interests. Preserving sovereignty was a crucial issue in a country that had been invaded by nearly every world power. This nationalist ideology was at the core of Díaz's generation—the president launched his political career as a hero of the war against the 1860s French occupation (Russell 2010, 188–213). The *científicos* formed a younger group that applied that principle to capital internationalisation and public finance. For this reason, Weiner (2000, 646) characterises them as "ambivalent internationalists," who opened the economy for nationalistic reasons. The most eminent *científico* was José Yves Limantour, Mexico's finance minister and chief debt negotiator between 1893 and 1911.

Gaining the Upper Hand: The 1899 Loan

The price of Mexico's debt increased as the silver crisis came to an end. The 6 per cent-type bonds were being traded around 90% of face value in 1895, and contemporaries expected that quotations would continue to rise. The improvement in credit conditions enabled the government to swap that debt for 5 per cent-type bonds. The Mexican negotiators spent the following four years negotiating the loan that would finance that conversion.

Bleichroeder was the first underwriter to approach the government. Its managers informed that the bank would be willing to participate in the conversion as soon as the market quoted the 6 per cent-type debt at 98% of par, which happened for the first time in July 1897.[7] Instead of rushing to issue the loan, Limantour and Sebastian Camacho, the Finance Ministry's agent in Europe, negotiated with as many underwriters as possible to pressure Bleichroeder to issue the new bonds at a discount between 95% and 96%, a level Limantour established as target.[8] Bleichroeder placed its first offer at 90–92%. Camacho classified the deal as "immoral," as he understood that the bank would "hold the bonds to sell them at a much higher price later on."[9]

Camacho suggested the inclusion of the "Paris market to balance the power that the Bleichroeder house has gained over the credit of the country."[10] Limantour contacted the Paris-based financier Noetzlin to intermediate with the French government a settlement over the *petit bleu*, the bonds issued during the French occupation and repudiated by President Juárez in the 1860s.[11] Differently from what had happened with the London debt, the French government rather than a body of bondholders imposed an embargo on Mexico after it defaulted on the *petit bleu*, and thus the access to the Paris market was a matter between states. Topik (2000) points out that the firm opposition to an agreement on that old debt in Mexico prevented both governments from reaching a solution. The *petit bleu* was a symbol of the French occupation. Limantour offered the purchase of guns from France in exchange for a settlement, but the deal was never signed.[12] That deadlock would prevent Mexico from issuing bonds in Paris until 1910.

Mexico also negotiated the inclusion of Dresdner, the underwriter of the 5% 1889 loan, in the conversion. The bank offered to convert the debt into 4% bonds, maintaining guarantees that involved the revenue

[7]The prices of the 1888, 1890 and 1893 bonds quoted in *The Investor's Monthly Manual* reached 98 of par in February, June and July 1897, respectively. As Bleichroeder referred to a conversion of the entire 6% debt, it follows that his house would launch the operation in July.

[8]*AJYL* Limantour to Camacho, 12 February 1896, 1st series, roll 3, no. 2271.

[9]*AJYL* Camacho to Limantour, 16 August 1896, 1st series, roll 3, no. 2275.

[10]*AJYL* Camacho to Limantour, 28 September 1895, 1st series, roll 3, no. 2578.

[11]*AJYL* Limantour to Noetzlin, 1 July 1898, 1st series, roll 8, no. 57732. See Chapter 6 for more on the *petit bleu*.

[12]*AJYL* Ibid.

of the state-owned Tehuantepec railway. Limantour considered the offer "too onerous to be accepted."[13] Dresdner then suggested the issuing of 5% bonds without any guarantees, which the minister agreed on the condition that the operation be integrated into the conversion the government was negotiating with Bleichroeder.[14] It is natural that the Mexicans preferred debt without guarantees; but unless they planned to default on the bonds (which was hardly the case), that should not have compensated for the issuing of 5 rather than 4 per cent-type bonds. The minister acted in that way to push for the formation of a large syndicate that would underwrite the new 5 per cent-type conversion bonds. The maintenance of the Tehuantepec debt at 5% was a condition for the introduction of Dresdner in that operation. The more banks that took part in that operation, the smaller the share Bleichroeder was going to underwrite.

Besides holding talks with Noetzlin and Dresdner, Limantour informally approached the London Rothschilds through Pearson, the contractor in charge of building the Tehuantepec railway. Rothschilds was not interested in participating in the conversion, although the bankers acknowledged that Mexico "was a coming country."[15] Finally, the minister searched for alternatives in New York. Mexican debt was also banned from Wall Street, although for a much simpler reason than the *petit bleu* in Paris: A US citizen had failed to convert old bonds in the 1885 settlement and presented the case that the country's debt was still on default. Limantour contacted an American consul who intervened in favour of the government at the New York Stock Exchange and arranged the clearance of Mexico's record in October 1898.[16] A few months later, in early 1899, the minister went to the USA to negotiate the conversion with JP Morgan and City Bank, which offered to underwrite 4 per cent-type bonds at a discount between 83% and 84%.[17]

The offer was better than the goal Limantour established three years earlier—more precisely, it resulted in a lower risk premium. This comparison appears in Table 7.2, which also reports the offer Bleichroeder presented to Mexico and the actual issuing conditions. Since all parts mentioned ranges of discounts, each offer has two different rates. The

[13] *AJYL* Limantour to Camacho, 16 December 1896, 1st series, roll 3, no. 2286.

[14] *AJYL* Limantour to Camacho, 7 April 1897, 1st series, roll 3, no. 2641.

[15] *AJYL* Pearson to Limantour, 4 June 1897, 1st series, roll 11, no. 2664.

[16] *AJYL* Andrew Barlow (US consul in Mexico) to Limantour and vice versa, 4 and 11 October 1898, 1st series, roll 2, no. 14479–80.

[17] *AJYL* Camacho to Díaz, 26 May 1899, 1st series, roll 3, no. 2301.

Table 7.2 Mexican 1899 loan: offered and issuing conditions (*Source* Offer conditions from AJYL; return on British consol and Mexican risk from *The Investor's Monthly Manual*)

	Interests (%)	*Discount (%)*	*Risk premium (%)*	*Risk premium (% Mexican risk)*
February 1996				
Limantour	5	95	2.74	75.53
		96	2.67	73.85
July 1897				
Bleichroeder	5	90	3.18	88.10
		92	3.05	84.45
May 1899				
JP Morgan	4	83	2.44	77.87
		84	2.38	75.82
June 1899				
Issuing	5	96	2.68	82.23

months referred to in the table are the dates when the quotes appeared in the correspondence. The only exception is the proposal from Bleichroeder, as the banker intended to launch the operation when the bonds it had underwritten reached 98% of par, which happened in July 1897, as explained above. There is no data on maturity in the material researched, and therefore all risk premiums have been calculated at 45 years, the maturity of the actual loan.

In spite of receiving a good offer in New York, Limantour left for Europe where he finally signed an agreement on the issuing of 5% bonds at 96% with a syndicate that included Bleichroeder, Dresdner, the British house Morgan Grenfell and, surprisingly, JP Morgan. According to Passananti (2006, 191), Bleichroeder arranged the introduction of JP Morgan to the operation to prevent Mexico from using the American offer as a bargaining tool when dealing with the Europeans. Archival material confirms that the Mexicans intended to do so. Just after crossing the Atlantic, Limantour received a cable from Díaz congratulating him on the results of the negotiations carried out in New York and hoping that the Europeans would present a proposal that "does not differ much from the average level until now established by the Americans."[18]

[18] *AJYL* Díaz to Limantour, 12 May 1899, 1st series, roll 5, no. 4707.

Similarly, Camacho declared that "the American offer surprised [the European banks] and will certainly force them to be more reasonable in their new proposals."[19]

Mexico did not launch the conversion at conditions similar to those offered in New York, but the operation was a success rather than the failure one would assume from Passananti (2006). Three points lead to this conclusion. Firstly, the Mexicans did not intend to have a US bank underwriting the whole conversion. According to Camacho, it "would not be convenient for the Mexican government if Europe completely lost her interest in the country's public securities."[20] Díaz celebrated the deal with a predominantly European syndicate in this tortuous but revealing passage:

> Your Excellency has done very well in refusing the volatile banks, taking for granted the real goal of your journey, and inspiring hope among those with the relative power to participate in what your Excellency may realize once in Europe.[21]

If the European-based syndicate was "those with relative power" and the American banks were "volatile," it follows that the issuing of the conversion bonds in Europe was the "true goal" Limantour was pursuing. Once the government finally issued the bonds, the president celebrated the "happy conversion of the debt," describing the results as a "solution that Your Excellency has so formidable arranged for the interests of the country."[22]

Weiner (2000) points out that Díaz and his high officials considered the growing US influence over the Mexican economy as a threat to sovereignty (Weiner 2000, 668). Had JP Morgan and City Bank underwritten the entire conversion, the Mexican debt would have become an American business. In other words, the inclusion of JP Morgan in the 1899 syndicate did not prevent Mexico from issuing the loan in New York, since that was not the government's plan from the start.

Secondly, the negotiation was not a failure because Bleichroeder increased the issuing discount to match Limantour's target. Had the

[19] *AJYL* Camacho to Limantour, 26 May 1899, 1st series, roll 3, no. 2301.

[20] Ibid.

[21] *AJYL* Díaz to Limantour, 12 May 1899, 1st series, roll 5, no. 4707.

[22] *AJYL* Díaz to Limantour, 15 June 1899, 1st series, roll 5, no. 4709.

government accepted the bank's average first offer (91%), it would have received a net revenue of £20.66 million instead of the actual £21.79 million. By delaying negotiations from July 1897 to June 1899, Mexico paid 6% interest on the 1888, 1890, and 1893 bonds, rather than 5% on the new ones during these two years. The outstanding Mexican 6 per cent-type debt was on average £19.96 million in that period, and thus the government paid extra £399,200 in interests.[23] Hence, the net gain from the negotiations was £735,800, a significant sum that corresponded to about 16% of the tax revenue collected in 1898–1899.[24] Finally, negotiators succeeded in diversifying credit sources, as the inclusion of Dresdner and JP Morgan in the syndicate reduced the relative role of Bleichroeder, which was in charge of underwriting 40.3% of the bonds, a large but not a majority share.[25]

Table 7.2 shows that the risk premium of every quote was lower than Mexican risk. As explained in the previous section, this is natural in conversions. It is noteworthy, however, that the risk premium at which the loan was issued was 82.23% of Mexican risk, which is close although below the range given in Bleichroeder's first offer (84.45–88.10%) and well above Limantour's target (73.85–75.53%). This comparison is relevant if one accepts the rather reasonable assumption that the bankers considered market conditions when deciding what rates to offer. At the beginning of negotiations, Bleichroeder would underwrite the bonds at a risk premium no less than 84% lower than Mexican risk. Mexico's target discount (95–96%) was too good in July 1897, but feasible in June 1899 because of the fall in Mexican risk and the negotiations during that period.

These figures suggest the following interpretation: Limantour and Camacho waited until the price of bonds increased significantly (and hence Mexican risk fell) to set the deal, understanding that the improvement in the credit Mexico had on the secondary market would make Bleichroeder more likely to issue the bonds at the rate they wanted. Meanwhile, they approached as many alternative underwriters as possible to put some extra pressure on the German bank to improve its offer. The Mexican negotiators arranged the deal at their best target discount,

[23] Sovereign debt stock from the *The Investor's Monthly Manual*.

[24] According to INEGI (1990, 627) the fiscal revenue for 1898–1899 was the equivalent of £4.7 million.

[25] Mexico (1925), Deuda Consolidada Exterior Mexicana 5% 1899.

below Bleichroeder's original range. Reputation among the bondholders was crucial, but negotiation also played a role.

The underwriters sold the 1899 bonds at a price 3.67% higher than the issuing discount. Had Bleichroeder underwritten the bond at 91% and sold them at the same price, the syndicate would have profited from an 8.67% margin, more than what it gained with the 1893 loan.[26] The remaining of this chapter shows how Limantour followed similar negotiation strategy—delaying decisions and involving different banks—in the 1900s to bargain for better terms and squeeze the underwriters' profitability, with even better results.

Mexico Goes to New York: The 1904 Loan

The 1900s was the golden age of the Porfiriato. Foreign trade boomed, fiscal accounts were sound, the country adopted the Gold Standard, and the government issued two loans at record low risk premiums in 1904 and 1910. The underwriters were Speyers, from the USA, and Paribas, from Paris. Both houses started doing business with the Mexican state at the turn of the century when they underwrote treasury notes that financed the nationalisation of railway companies. The notes were short term, and the banks offered their services to redeem them with the issuing of a long-term loan, which Speyers underwrote in 1904.

Noetzlin acted as intermediary in the talks between the government and Paribas. In March 1903, he communicated to Limantour that the bank, in association with the New York house Kuhn Loeb, was willing to underwrite 5% bonds of 40 years maturity, totalling 125 million francs (the equivalent of £5 million). Mexico would receive 77.5% of the loan after Paribas used a share of the credit to redeem the *petit bleu*. Noetzlin estimated the outstanding *petit bleu* in 3 million francs, the equivalent of 2.4% of the proposed loan.[27] The correspondence does not include figures on the commission and the issuing discount rates, but assuming that the former was 1%, the rate charged on the 1899 loan, it follows that the latter was 80%. This results in a 3.4% risk premium, far above Mexican risk, which was 1.8%.

[26]Calculated from the *The Interstor's Monthly Manual* and Mexico (1925).

[27]*AHP* Noetzlin to Limantour, 18 March 1903, Projet d'Emprunt Mexicain, *AHP*, 11/DFOM-221/1138.

Limantour considered the deal "impracticable" and the cost of opening the market in Paris "exorbitant." He asserted that "if the French market appears so disadvantageous, Mexico would definitively renounce it." The minister asked Noetzlin to reconsider "the parsimony with which you regard the possible value of Mexican bonds" and declared Mexico open for future offers as long as these included "much better prices" and an "important reduction in expenses." In that same cable, Limantour informed Noetzlin that "a US bank" would launch a similar loan at a 4.5% interests and a 92% discount, which is equivalent to a 1.9% risk premium.[28] The financier replied that a "reduction in expenses would perhaps be possible," but his proposal would not match the offer from New York, whose market was "not trustworthy" and "full of juvenile spirits."[29]

Noetzlin became more precise once it was clear that the competitor was Speyer: He described James Speyer, the house's director, as "pushy, exigent, and perhaps a bit full of petulance."[30] The financier invited Bleichroeder to join Paribas' syndicate, consolidating a European group. Bleichroeder's director accepted the invitation, as he "did not love Speyer very much."[31] The syndicate presented a new offer, raising the discount rate (not including the conversion of the *petit bleu*) to 83.5%. Limantour demanded a further increase to 86%, and Noetzlin confidentially established with his partners a limit of 85%.[32]

In October 1904, a few weeks before the issuing of the loan, Speyer presented a second quote to Limantour, reducing the interest rate from 4.5% to 4% and setting the discount at "somewhat more than 83%."[33] The minister considered the deal unsatisfactory because it did not include any arrangement for the *petit bleu*.[34] He believed that the underwriters were supposed to "arrange official quotes on the Paris Stock Exchange for the Mexican public security" and "deliver to the Government the petit papers that for so long have been an obstacle or

[28] *AHP* Limantour to Noetzlin, 7 April 1903, 11/DFOM-221/1138.

[29] *AHP* Noetzlin to Limantour, 30 April 1903, 11/DFOM-221/1138.

[30] *AHP* Noetzlin to Limantour, 15 April 1904, 11/DFOM-221/1138.

[31] *AHP* Noetzlin to Schiff (Kuhn Loeb), 2 July 1904, 11/DFOM-221/1138.

[32] *AHP* Noetzlin to Schiff, August 1904, 11/DFOM-221/1138.

[33] *AJYL* Speyer to Limantour, 5 October 1904, 2nd series, roll 26, no. 11.

[34] *AJYL* Limantour to Speyer, 8 October 1904, 2nd series, roll 26, no. 11.

pretext to prevent the admission of such securities."[35] Limantour pressured the banks to "take the entire loan, including all expenses and the petit papers."[36] That was valid for both Speyer and Paribas, although Noetzlin insisted that Mexico rather than the underwriters was supposed to "make a sacrifice to open up Paris."[37]

Topik (2000, 732) argues that the minister was inflexible on the *petit bleu* to balance the opposition from more nationalistic members of the Mexican establishment, who condemned his French origins. The correspondence researched for this book supports this interpretation: A Paribas agent informed Noetzlin that Limantour would not accept the bank's offer because of "personal politics."[38]

Noetzlin increased the discount rate to 85%, the upper limit established by the members of the Paribas-Bleichroeder syndicate. Limantour replied in a rather odd fashion: He proposed the inclusion of Speyer in the syndicate formed by Paribas, Kuhn Loeb and Bleichroeder.[39] After fostering competition to improve borrowing conditions, the minister promoted cooperation to diversify credit sources.

Passananti (2006, 199) acknowledges that Limantour stimulated competition and argues that he was successful because Speyers did not want to join Paribas' syndicate after being invited by Noetzlin. In contrast, the evidence analysed here suggests that, after improving the bank's offers, Limantour was also in favour of a larger syndicate to limit the role of any individual bank. Moreover, it does not seem the case that the European-based group was willing to cooperate: Noetzlin declared that Paribas would not accept Speyers in the operation because its partner Kuhn Loeb refused to share the role of underwriter in New York.[40]

If the promotion of cooperation after one year of competition was Mexico's final goal, the plan backfired. However, the final result turned out to be positive: In order to secure exclusivity, Speyer increased the discount rate at which it would underwrite the 4 per cent-type bonds from 83% to

[35] *AHP* Limantour to Noetzlin, 2 August 1904, 11/DFOM-221/1138.

[36] *AHP* Limantour to Notzlin, 5 September 1904, 11/DFOM-221/1138.

[37] *AHP* Noetzlin to Limantour, 8 September 1904, 11/DFOM-221/1138.

[38] *AHP* Moret (Paribas) to Noetzlin, 11 October 1904, 11/DFOM-221/1138.

[39] *AHP* Noetzlin to Moret, 6 October 1904, Projet d'Emprunt Mexicain, 11/DFOM-221/1138.

[40] *AHP* Noetzlin to Moret, 6 October 1904, 11/DFOM-221/1138.

Table 7.3 Mexican 1904 loan: offered and issuing conditions (*Source* Offer conditions from AJYL; return on British consol and Mexican risk from *The Investor's Monthly Manual*)

	Interest (%)	*Discount (%)*	*Maturity (years)*	*Risk premium (%)*	*Risk premium (% Mexican risk)*
March 1903					
Paribas	5.0	80.0	40	3.35	181.98
Speyers	4.5	92.0	50	1.89	102.52
August 1904					
Paribas	5.0	83.5	40	3.28	161.93
Limantour	5.0	86.0	40	3.09	152.50
October 1904					
Paribas	5.0	85.0	40	3.16	160.64
Speyers	4.0	83.0	50	2.08	105.89
Issuing (Speyers)	4.0	89.0	50	1.73	87.72

89%.[41] Limantour welcomed the proposal but did not accept it immediately. He declared that his government would insist in pursuing a broad European-American syndicate unless Speyer paid for the redemption of the *petit bleu*. The banker regretted such "threats" but "hope[d] your Government will sell us [the] whole loan." Speyer then agreed to "use our best effort" to buy back the *petit bleu* in Paris with his bank's resources.[42]

Table 7.3 lists the quotes Paribas and Speyer presented during the negotiations. It reports the discount rates Noetzlin proposed not considering the cost of converting the *petit bleu*—that is, the discount at which Paribas' syndicate was ready to issue the loan rather than the revenue Mexico was going to receive. As explained above, Noetzlin mentioned that Paribas intended to issue 40-year bonds. Speyer never referred to maturity but ended up underwriting a 50-year loan in 1904. Thus, risk premiums have been calculated according to these two pieces of

[41] *AJYL* Speyer to Limantour, 14 October 1904, 2nd series, roll 26, no. 11.

[42] *AJYL* James Speyer to Limantour, 15 October 1904, 2nd series, roll 26, no. 11.

information: 40-year maturity for Paribas and 50 years for Speyers.[43] Limantour placed a counter-offer in August 1904 based on a proposition from Paribas, and thus the risk premium applied to that rate has been calculated at 40-year maturity.

Paribas offered to issue the bonds at a higher risk premium than Speyers, which is natural given the difference between their respective statuses: a European bank representing a relatively established syndicate and an American house that was about to issue the first foreign loan in Wall Street's history. The rates from Paribas were substantially higher than Mexican risk, which was less the case with Speyers, indicating that the Europeans intended to profit more than the Americans from the subsequent sale of bonds on the secondary market. Competition forced Paribas to increase discount rates, resulting in lower risk premiums. In the end, Speyers made an excellent offer, accepting to issue the bonds below Mexican risk.

Yet Speyer profited from a 5% price run-up. According to Topik (2000, 468), that bank spent 1.7 million francs (the equivalent of £68,000 or 0.83% of the loan) redeeming the *petit bleu* (Topik 2000, 468). Thus, the net gain was 4.17%, not far from the 1899 loan. Profitability reflected the market's appetite for Mexican securities, a consequence of the expansion in world liquidity during the *Belle Époque* as well as the orthodox economic policies implemented in Mexico—the country went on gold in May 1905, one month before the 1904 bonds appeared on the market.[44] The fact that Speyers managed to profit from its aggressive offer reveals that Paribas's syndicate expected a very high rate of return. Limantour squeezed the bank's profitability, and thanks to the country's good credit, was able to pressure Speyers to improve its offer to a level Mexico would not refuse.

[43]Similar results hold if maturity (the only piece of information not completely available) was the same in the proposals Paribas and Speyer presented to Mexico. At 50 instead of 40 years, the risk premiums applied to Paribas' offers would have been 3.28%, 3.22% and 3.11%, which are slightly lower than those calculated at 40 years but still way higher than Speyers' rates.

[44]See Sotelo (2009, 18, 19) for more on the adoption of the Gold Standard in Mexico.

Porfiriato's Finest Hour: The 1910 Loan

Why did James Speyer decide to propose such an aggressive deal in 1904, which included the issuing of a loan below the market rate and the redemption of the *petit bleu* in Paris? The banker probably expected a rise in the bonds' price once Mexico went on gold, which actually happened. Topik (1993, 466) presents an additional reason that involves a conflict of interest: the loan allowed Speyers to buy back the railway treasuries issued in the previous years and sell them at higher prices to the government.

Another non-excluding explanation is that the operation was an entrance door into Mexican finance, which was crucial because Speyers intended to become Mexico's patron bank. In 1906, James Speyer proposed to convert the 1899 bonds in an operation that would have turned the entire Mexican debt into his own business. Limantour declined the offer, claiming that the 1899 loan contract prevented a conversion at par in the following ten years. The government was allowed to buy the bonds above face value, but bondholders could refuse to participate, a risk that the minister considered too high unless other underwriters were involved in the operation. He suggested Paribas as an associate, attempting once more to build a transatlantic syndicate.[45] I found no response in the archives researched, which suggests that Speyer did not consider the proposition.

Three years later, when the government could already convert the bonds at par, Speyer proposed a second deal, according to which it would underwrite 4 per cent-type bonds at a 90% discount. Assuming the same 50-year maturity of the 1904 loan, the risk premium is 1.54%. The bank proposed a 2.5% commission rate, against the 1% charged in 1904.[46] Limantour characterised the deal as premature and declared that he would only agree if "expenses [were] reduced to a minimum."[47] The banker decreased the commission to 1%, which was not enough to convince the minister.[48] A few months later, the underwriters of the 1899 loan—Bleichroeder, Dresdner Bank, Morgan Grenfell and JP Morgan—proposed to issue the conversion at 4.5% interest and a 90% discount. Limantour instructed Hugo Scherer, who was serving as the

[45] *AJYL* Limantour to Speyer, 14 February 1906, 2nd series, roll 38, no. 9.

[46] *AJYL* Speyer to Limantour, 9 February 1909, 2nd series, roll 58, no. 9.

[47] *AJYL* Limantour to Speyer, 10 February 1909, 2nd series, roll 58, no. 9.

[48] *AJYL* Speyer to Limantour, 20 February 1909, 2nd series, roll 58, no. 9.

Finance Ministry's agent in Europe, to insist on setting the interest rate at 4%, claiming that the Mexican press was launching a campaign against the operation.[49]

For the second time in five years, Limantour contacted Noetzlin to include French banks in debt negotiations. Noetzlin argued that Mexico needed the liquidity available in France if it was to issue the conversion bonds at a 4% interest rate. He suggested the introduction of a pool of French banks—Paribas, Crédit Lyonnais, Société Générale and Comptoir National d'Escompte—into the 1899 syndicate.[50] It was the third time Noetzlin attempted to coordinate the underwriting of Mexican bonds in Paris, but now the *petit bleu* was out of the way. The minister welcomed the proposal but regretted that he could not impose the inclusion of those houses on Bleichroeder and its partners. Limantour devised an astute strategy: he was going to "ask too high a price for the new bonds, so the [1899] syndicate will be practically forced [...] to reach an agreement with the major French houses."[51] That turned out to be a favourable decision. The 1899 syndicate accepted the inclusion of the French banks, which underwrote 42.5% of the loan.[52] This larger syndicate lowered the interest rate to 4% and raised the discount to 94.75%, the final issuing price.

Table 7.4 shows that the 1899 syndicate intended to issue the conversion bonds above Mexican risk. Limantour did not accept that offer, demanding a discount that resulted in a risk premium below the market rate. The bargaining was so effective that the loan was issued at the lowest risk premium since Mexico returned to the market, not only in absolute terms but also relative to Mexican risk, even though the latter was at a record low.[53]

The 1910 loan was issued at a 94.75% discount and first appeared on the market at 96.38% of face value. This results in a 1.63% price run-up, which is ten times lower than that applied to the first Porfirian loan, issued two decades earlier.[54] It consisted in a remarkable success as long as Mexico's two goals in debt negotiations are concerned: the reduction

[49] *AJYL* Limantour to Scherer, 16 August 1909, 2nd series, roll 60, no. 17.

[50] *AJYL* Noetzlin to Limantour, 15 August 1909, 2nd series, roll 60, no. 17.

[51] *AJYL* Limantour to Noetzlin, 2 October 1909, 2nd series, roll 60, no. 17.

[52] Mexico (1925) Deuda Exterior Mexicana 4% Oro de 1910.

[53] The issuing risk premiums were 82.23% and 87.72% of Mexican Risk in the 1899 and 1904 loans, respectively, against 76.65% for the 1910 loan. Calculated from Mexico (1925) and *The Investor's Monthly Manual*.

[54] See Chapter 6.

Table 7.4 Mexican 1910 loan: offered and issuing conditions (*Source* Offer conditions from AJYL; return on British consol and Mexican risk from New York Stock Exchange and *The Investor's Monthly Manual*)

	Interests (%)	*Discount (%)*	*Maturity (years)*	*Risk premium (%)*	*Risk premium (% Mexican risk)*
February 1909					
Speyer	4.0	90.00	50	1.54	88.43
August 1909					
1899 Syndicate	4.5	90.00	35	2.15	129.28
Limantour	4.0	90.00	35	1.61	96.80
June 1910					
Final offer	4.0	94.75	35	1.27	76.65

of borrowing costs and the diversification of credit sources. It is striking that the government borrowed so cheaply just a few months before the outbreak of the Revolution that deposed Porfirio Díaz and subsequently destroyed the state established under his rule. The debt went on default in 1914. The choice of not having a patron became problematic in the crisis that followed the Revolution, the topic of Chapter 8.

Conclusion

The autocratic Porfirian regime delivered sound public finance, which officials considered a precondition for sovereignty. The government benefited from a growing economy, but its commitment to raise taxes and its active role in negotiating sovereign debt also played a role in improving fiscal accounts. Minister Limantour skilfully explored the competition of emerging banks from continental Europe and the USA to bargain for good borrowing conditions. He was successful to the point that Mexico nearly borrowed as if it had direct access to the secondary market, issuing bonds without paying for the underwriters' services. That is the reason why the 1899, 1904 and particularly the 1910 loans were issued at risk premiums significantly below Mexican risk.

Negotiations were successful because the government was powerful vis-à-vis the banks, a consequence of its nearly acquired reputation. Mexico was in a virtuous cycle: Cheap borrowing strengthened fiscal accounts, which increased the power of negotiators to improve borrowing conditions even more. That was only possible because the Mexicans consistently refused to have a patron bank. Credit diversification enabled the government to negotiate loans with different underwriters but reduced the probability of rescue loans in the future, which turned out to be a problem in the turbulent 1910s.

References

Archival Sources

AJYL Archivo José Yves Limantour, Condumex, Mexico City.
Correspondencias, 1st and 2nd series.
AHP Archive Historique Paribas, Paris.
Projet d'Emprunt Mexicain, 11/DFOM.
BC Bleichroeder Collection, Baker Library, Boston.
1983 Loan folder.
Jewish Affairs folder.

Official and Contemporary Sources

Bulletin de la Côte

INEGI. 1990. *Estadísticas históricas de México.* Mexico City: Instituto Nacional de Estadística, Geografía e Informática.

Mexico. 1925. *Colección de leyes y disposiciones relacionadas con la deuda exterior de México.* Mexico City: Secretaría de Hacienda y Crédito Público.

———. *Cuentas del Tesoro Federal formada por la Tesoreria General de La Federación.* Mexico City: Tipografía de la Oficina Impresora del Timbre.

——— *Memoria de Hacienda y Crédito Público.* Mexico City: Tipografía de la Oficina Impresora del Timbre.

The Economist.

The Investor's Monthly Manual.

Secondary Sources

Carmagnani, Marcello. 1994. *Estado y mercado: la economía pública del liberalismo mexicano, 1850–1911.* Mexico City: El Colegio de México.

Catão, Luís A. V. 1998. "Mexico and Export-Led Growth: The Porfirian Period Revisited." *Cambridge Journal of Economics* 22 (1):59–78.

Ficker, Sandra K. 2002. "Nuevas series del comercio exterior de México, 1870–1929." *Revista de Historia Económica* 20 (2):213–70.

Mitchener, Kris J., and Marc D. Weidenmier. 2007. "The Baring Crisis and the Great Latin American Meltdown of the 1890s." Working Paper 13403. National Bureau of Economic Research.

Passananti, Thomas P. 2006. "Conflicto y cooperación financiera en la Belle Époque: Bancos alemanes en el Porfiriato tardio." In *Mexico y la economia atlantica siglos XVIII–XX/ Mexico and the Atlantic economy XVIII–XX centuries*, edited by Sandra Kuntz Ficker and Horst Pietschmann, 173–203. Mexico City: El Colegio de México.

Rosales, Ricardo S. 1996. "Crisis financieras durante el Porfiriato, algunas notas para su interpretación." In *Pasado y presente de la deuda externa de México*, edited by Jaime E. Reyno, 98–130. Mexico City: UNAM.

Rosenzweig, Fernando. 2005. "El desarrollo económico de México de 1877 a 1911." In *Historia económica de México*, edited by Enrique Cárdenas, 43–67. Mexico City: Fondo de Cultura Económica.

Russell, Philip L. 2010. *The History of Mexico: From Pre-Conquest to Present.* London: Routledge.

Sotelo, Romero, and María Eugenia. 2009. "Patrón oro y estabilidad cambiaria en México, 1905–1910." *América Latina en la historia económica. Revista de Investigación* 32:81–109.

Tomz, Michael. 2012. *Reputation and International Cooperation: Sovereign Debt Across Three Centuries.* Princeton: Princeton University Press.

Topik, Steven C. 1993. "Controversia crediticia: los "azulitos" del periodo de Maximiliano." In *Los negocios y las ganancias de la colonia al México moderno*, edited by Leonor Ludlow and Jorge S. Riquer, 445–70. Mexico City: Instituto Mora.

Topik, Steven C. 2000. "When Mexico Had the Blues: A Transatlantic Tale of Bonds, Bankers, and Nationalists, 1862–1910." *The American Historical Review* 105 (3):714–38.

Weiner, Richard. 2000. "Battle for Survival: Porfirian Views of the International Marketplace." *Journal of Latin American Studies* 32 (3):645–70.

Weller, Leonardo. 2015. "Government versus Bankers: Sovereign Debt Negotiations in Porfirian Mexico, 1888–1910." *Journal of Economic History* 75 (4):1030–57.

CHAPTER 8

The Loans of the Revolution: Mexico, 1911–1914

The Mexican Revolution deposed Porfirio Díaz in 1911. Once in office, the movement's leader Francisco Madero (1911–1913) failed to reach a compromise with popular rebels on land reform. The insurgents took in arms against Madero, who was assassinated in a counter-revolution led by General Huerta (1913–1914). Huerta imposed a dictatorship and waged war on the insurgents and constitutionalist forces, who took Mexico City in 1914. The state collapsed and the country remained without a central government for three years. Madero and Huerta administrations borrowed abroad to combat the insurgents. Speyer issued two short-term loans for £2 million in 1912 and 1913, and a large syndicate headed by Paribas issued a loan for £6 million in 1913. This chapter assesses why foreign bankers decided to lend money to a government involved in a total civil war.

Inside information and conflict of interest explain why Paribas accepted to underwrite the 1913 loan. The bank had access to first-hand sources that were more accurate than the over-optimistic press. Paribas forced the government to issue the bonds at conditions that were disproportionably expensive and sold them at a 6% margin on the secondary market. The credit enabled the government to continue honouring its obligations for a few months, during which Paribas sold its entire Mexican portfolio without realising losses. Another reason that explains the loans was the Nacional railway, Mexico's larger state-owned line. The lending prevented the company from defaulting on its debt, which both Paribas and Speyers had underwritten in the 1900s.

L. Weller, *Sovereign Debt Crises and Negotiations in Brazil and Mexico, 1888-1914*, https://doi.org/10.1007/978-3-319-73633-4_8

Paribas was not highly exposed to Mexico, which explains why it did not grant a rescue loan. The bank had only issued one Mexican loan in 1910, and the bulk of its businesses in France did not depend on its reputation as an underwriter of sovereign debt. Speyers was more exposed but did not have the means to rescue Mexico. The outcome could have been different had the government handed a monopoly on its debt to a patron bank during the Porfirio.

The Mexican Revolution

The Mexican Revolution swiftly toppled the long-lasting authoritarian rule of Porfirio Díaz. Decades of peace and stability had alienated social classes and political groups. Francisco Madero's non-re-election campaign formed a wide revolutionary front in face of which Díaz had no option but to resign without offering much resistance.

Indigenous peasants formed the most excluded group of the Porfiriato. The Porfirian government privatised public land, dissolving an arrangement that had protected the subsistence of native peoples and their descendants since colonial times. Privatisation started during the administration of Lerdo de Tejada (1872–1876), but it was under Díaz that the state sold most of its properties. The share of communal land in the Mexican territory fell from about 40% in the 1860s to only 5% in 1911 (Trigger et al. 1996, 328).

The peasants who lived in public land applied traditional farming methods. More productive, the new farms contributed to the growth in merchandise exports and liberated labour for the also dynamic mining and industrial sectors. Rural Mexico experienced technological change, but labour relations continued backwards. Most new farms adopted the traditional system of peonage in which workers laboured to pay debts (Catão 1998).

Land privatisation and a repressive labour regime created the conditions for the formation of rebellious movements in the countryside. Emiliano Zapata was perhaps the most notorious rural insurgent leader. He headed an armed group in the state of Morelos that took in arms to fight for land reform in 1907 (Leal 1986, 21–22). Around the same period, mine workers launched a wave of strikes against poor working conditions, which had not improved significantly in spite of the development of that sector in the previous decades. Similar movements appeared in the growing industrial sector. Government forces brutally repressed the strikes in mines and factories, which divided opinions among the still small but growing urban middle class (Knight 1986, 21–22; Gómez-Galvarriato 2003).

The opposition to Díaz was also political. Porfirian state concentrated power around the president, reducing the autonomy of local governments at the state and municipal levels. That was one of the most significant victories of the regime: The dictator unified the country after decades during which regional elites ruled territories independently from the central state. Demanding freedom in municipalities (*municipio libre*) in the Mexican north, the insurgents Pancho Villa and Pascual Orozco declared war against the dictator. Members of the establishment also condemned the regime. The former governor and senator Venustiano Carranza joined the opposition after losing a state election in Coahuila, also in the north. Carranza claimed that Díaz rigged the election to favour one of his protégés, in a typical development of the Porfiriato (Joseph and Buchenau 2013, 38–43).

Further, a generation clash explains the fall of Díaz. Economic growth did not prevent the young members of the wealthy and educated families from resenting the lack of participation in the political game. This was the case of Francisco Madero, a landowner who was also from the state of Coahuila. Born in 1873, Madero shared little in common with those in power. By the time the Revolution broke out, all members of the cabinet were over sixty and the dictator was eighty years old. Madero published a non-re-election manifesto and ran for office against Díaz in 1910. He left for the USA after being arrested and quickly released. The different groups that opposed Díaz supported Madero's manifesto. The revolutionaries crossed the border and took Ciudad Juárez, galvanising the insurgents that operated elsewhere in the country. The dictator resigned and went into exile in May 1911. Madero was elected president later that year in perhaps Mexico's first free and fair election (Womack 1984, 83; Katz 2004).

Madero launched the Revolution to widen political representation rather than to redistribute wealth. His administration was pro-business. Shortly after taking office, the new president offered a banquet to members of the financial elite of Mexico City and created a trade agency in the USA. A third of his cabinet had served in the also pro-business Porfirian state. Exports and foreign investment in railways increased in 1911 and 1912, which is striking given that years' radical political changes (Reyes 1996, 70–108). External factors partially explain such positive results: The economy was recovering from the world crisis of 1908, which had severely hit Mexico. Yet the continuation of economic policy also conditioned the positive economic indicators of the early revolutionary period (Sánchez 2006, 33–66).

Madero's friendly approach to business promoted growth but created a political deadlock. Zapata would only demobilise his troops if the new administration pushed for land reform, which Madero would not do. Zapata rose against the new government, starting a campaign that received the support of Orozco. The strong man in the Army, General Huerta crushed Orozco's troops in mid-1912. The fight continued as Villa, until then a follower of Orozco but a supporter of Madero, built an alliance with Zapata. That marked the beginning of the civil war that was going to last for five more years (Knight 1986, 294).

Madero became trapped between two opposing forces when General Huerta switched sides to launch a counter-revolution with Félix Díaz, the nephew of Porfirio who had returned from exile (Garfias 1997, 77–93). The US ambassador Henry Wilson mediated a deal according to which Huerta would depose Madero and call for elections. Felix Díaz would be elected president and open the country to American oil companies. Madero had favoured British companies to balance the growing influence of the USA in the national economy—a strategy similar to the one Díaz and Limantour had implemented when dealing with foreign bankers, as seen in Chapter 7 (Katz 2003, 104–8; Womack 1984, 90–95).

Huerta's troops captured Mexico City and assassinated Madero in February 1913. Instead of calling for elections, Huerta dissolved Congress and ruled as a dictator. His forces combated the insurgents under the command of Villa and Zapata and the loosely defined Constitutionalist Army led by Caranza. In an unexpected move, Huerta kept the country closed to US oil companies. The measure generated fury on the northern side of the border. American companies started to finance the constitutionalists, and President Woodrow Wilson refused to recognise Huerta administration. The diplomatic crisis escalated to the point that the US Navy took the port city of Veracruz in April 1914. Besides reducing tax revenue, the invasion also made it more difficult for the Army to import guns and ammunition from Europe. The rebels finally deposed Huerta in July, but the conflict was far from over. Villa and Zapata revolted against the more conservative leaders of the Revolution such as

Table 8.1 Mexico's fiscal data, 1907–1913 (million Mexican pesos) (*Source Cuentas del Tesoro Federal*)

	Expenditure				*Tax revenue*	*Primary balance*
	Defence	*Domestic debt*	*Sovereign debt*	*Total*		
1907–1908	17.57	7.76	18.46	104.88	111.81	33.15
1908–1909	18.18	7.64	18.23	104.41	98.78	20.24
1909–1910	19.18	7.87	18.39	107.46	106.33	25.13
1910–1911	24.62	7.66	21.29	113.49	111.14	26.61
1911–1912	33.33	7.86	17.84	119.78	105.21	11.12
1912–1913	49.68	9.12	40.99	153.33	120.96	17.74

Carranza. The state collapsed and the civil war lasted until 1917 (Beller 2008, 112–20; Katz 2004; Joseph and Buchenau 2013).

The Fiscal Impact of the Revolution

The Revolution took place in a benign context of economic growth and relatively sound fiscal accounts. The rise in trade after the end of the 1907–1908 crisis in the USA increased tax receipts, which compensated for the growing military expenditure in the first year of the Revolution. Table 8.1 shows that the government ran a large primary balance that covered the services due on the sovereign debt in 1910–1911.

The deterioration of political conditions severely compromised fiscal accounts in the following two years. The conflict increased the defence budget even further and slowed economic activity, with negative impacts on tax revenue. These developments had negative consequences to the banking sector—the insurgents looted banks, forcing many branches to close their doors (Gómez-Galvarriato and Recio 2007; Maurer 2002, 139). The primary surplus could not cover the services due on the sovereign debt in 1911–1912. The government borrowed £2 million from Speyer in mid-1912. The loan had a one-year maturity, which explains the rise in the cost of servicing the debt in the following fiscal year as shown in Table 8.1. The Treasury was in a state of bankruptcy by the time Huerta took office, just as the government needed more resources to fight the rebels.

Nevertheless, the comparison between primary balance and obligations on the public debt underestimates the full extent of the fiscal crisis. Rebels sabotaged railway lines, targeting the state-owned Ferrocarril Nacional, a major line that linked the centre to the north of the country. Profits slumped by 82% between 1911–1912 and 1912–1913 and the company lacked funds to honour £2.72 million due on its foreign debt in 1913.[1] The government guaranteed those bonds, which, together with the services on the domestic and external debt, resulted in a total financial obligation of £7.8 million due in 1912–1913. Discounting for the primary surplus, the government lacked the equivalent of £6.1 million.[2]

Mexico would have most likely defaulted had it not issued a £6 million loan in June 1913. The underwriters were Crédit Comptoir, Société Générale, Bleichroeder, Deutsche Bank, Dresdner, Morgan Grenfell, JP Morgan, Kuhn Loeb and Paribas, the latter of which was the head of the syndicate. The list includes all the underwriters of Porfirian debt with the only exception of Speyer, which rolled over its £2 million short-term credit in August.

Huerta administration borrowed a total of £8 million, which was enough to cover the financial obligations due in 1913. But the credit was insufficient to meet the growing needs of the Army. The government minted copper coins, which depreciated the peso vis-à-vis the dollar by 34% in that year. Mexico left the Gold Standard after nearly a decade of exchange rate stability (Reyes 1996, 140–42; Sánchez 2006, 86–88). The president then pressured local bankers for credit, and troops took the Banco de Morelos (Maurer 2002, 142). The government finally defaulted on its debt in the first half of 1914. All that happened before the outbreak of the First World War, which means that internal affairs drove the debt crisis of the Revolution.

The 1913 Loan

Why did Paribas and its fellow syndicate members underwrite loans to revolutionary Mexico? One possible explanation is exposure. These bankers indeed preferred that the government continued to honour the debts they had underwritten in the past. As discussed in Chapter 2,

[1] *AHP* 11/DFOM-211/821 and 1138.

[2] Fiscal data from Mexico (1925) and *Cuentas del Tesoro Federal*; exchange rate from INEGI (1990).

banks were better underwriters the less their clients defaulted. Yet reputation does not explain Paribas' loan for three reasons. Firstly, Mexico lacked a patron bank, which enabled the government to negotiate good deals but left it without a safety net during the Revolution. Paribas underwrote Mexican bonds only once, in 1910.[3] Its status was not strongly linked to Mexico as Rothschilds' brand was to Brazil.

Secondly, the rescuing hypothesis is flawed because the funds involved in the 1913 loan did not cover Mexico's financial and military needs. The Mexicans tried to borrow as much as possible. Arguing that "the new government was strong and serious, fortunately inspired by the methods of Porfirio Díaz," Finance Minister Toribio Obregón proposed a loan for £20 million.[4] Had the bankers agreed to that figure, the government would have counted with £12 million after honouring all its financial obligations due in 1912–1913. Assuming that the exchange rate remained stable, that sum would have been enough to cover an extra year of debt services (both external and domestic) and to raise military expenditure by a factor of 2.6 in 1913–1914.

The underwriters did not even consider the proposal. The government subsequently released a statement communicating that it was going to issue a loan for £11 million.[5] That would have been enough to cover payments due in 1912–1913 and 1913–1914 and to increase the military budget by 8.5%. The Mexicans would have likely used most of the funds to fight the rebels. Had the loan only financed war, the defence budget would have increased by 87%. In other words, this more modest loan could have either protected the creditors or the regime, but not all of them altogether. It is not clear how much the members of the syndicate were aware of these figures, but their choice of lending only £6 million suggests that they were not primarily committed to the future of Huerta's government.

Finally, and most importantly, preventing a default was not among the bankers' priority because the loan was expensive. Paribas's syndicate underwrote a 6 per cent-type loan at a 90% discount and ten years maturity, during which the government was entitled to repay the principal annually at par. This results in a 4.08% risk premium, which is lower than the rate applied to most of the early Porfirian loans, issued from

[3] See Table 1.2 for the list of Mexican loans and its underwriters.

[4] *AHP* Simon to Paribas, 13 March 1913, 11/DFOM-221/27.

[5] *AHB* C. 1.11, 1913 loan folder.

1888 to 1893. However, the 1913 loan was issued 76% above Mexican risk, which makes it the most expensive operation to that date vis-à-vis the credit the government had on the market.[6] The bankers that underwrote the operation were aware that the government was accepting rather adverse terms. Morgan Grenfell, a member of the syndicate, recognised that the lending was "too severe a burden on the Government."[7]

Paribas, Asymmetry of Information and Conflict of Interest

The 1913 loan was small and expensive because the underwriters understood that Mexico's politics were dangerously volatile. Horace Finaly, from Paribas, informed his fellow syndicate members that the "general political and financial situation is very difficult." Paribas would only underwrite the loan at a "minimum risk" for the underwriters.[8] The operation had to be arranged "in our favour" because of the "terrible political circumstances" in the country. Finaly quoted "our representative in Mexico,"[9] who fed Paribas with reports such as the following:

> The political situation is (…) obscure because the country is still infested by rebellious bands while General Huerta is only president of the republic in a provisory character with Félix Díaz as concurrent, and no one knows how that will end.[10]

This realistic insight contrasts with how the general public viewed Mexico. The outbreak of the Revolution at first did not disrupt the economic

[6] The ratios between the issuing risk premium applied to the Porfirian loans and Mexican risk in the month of issue are: 1.07 (1889 loan), 1.24 (1890 loan), 0.91 (1893 loan), 0.83 (1899 loan), 0.88 (1904 loan) and 0.73 (1910 loan). The 1888 loan is not applicable because there was not a market for non-defaulted Mexican debt when it was issued. Data from Mexico (1925) and *The Investor's Monthly Manual*. See Fig. 1.2 for a visual comparison.

[7] *AHP* Morgan Grenfell to Finaly (Paribas), 22 April 1913, 11/DFOM-221/27.

[8] *AHP* Paribas to Simon, 12 March 1913, 11/DFOM-221/27.

[9] *AHP* Paribas to Bleichroeder, 30 April 1913, 11/DFOM-221/27.

[10] *AHP* Rengnet (Paribas, from Mexico) to Paribas, 17 April 1913, 11/DFOM-221/27.

order. The relative peace and growth when the regime changed influenced how the international press interpreted subsequent events. Shortly before Madero's assassination, *The Statist* published that "the reports from Mexico are now of a much satisfactory character, and an improvement in the trade and prosperity of the country is anticipated."[11] Along the same lines, *The Times* printed that "the country has been shaken and torn by revolutions and general disorder (but) has, nevertheless, overcome all these difficulties." The newspaper stressed that "the output figures point rather to an increase than a decrease."[12]

A similarly optimistic view appeared in the British Parliamentary Papers, according to which the growth in exports was "very remarkable, when it is considered that conditions in many parts of the country were the reverse of peaceful." The report then conjectured that "with the re-establishment of peace in the country foreign trade may be expected to increase enormously."[13]

Figure 8.1 measures how *The Times* described Mexico's political development. It shows the number of positive and negative reports the newspaper published on the country every month. Reports are defined as good or bad depending on the words that composed their headlines. Words that refer to political stability such as "pacification" and "rebel's defeat" are good news. The words "turmoil" and "revolt" are examples of terms that appear in bad news. Headlines seldom contained both positive and negative words. Such reports have been excluded.

The Times published a series of bad news in late 1910 and early 1911, when Madero deposed Díaz. It then printed some positive reports in May 1911, mentioning an "armistice." The newspaper went quiet on Mexico until it briefly reported the rising of the insurgents in early 1912 and Huerta's coup in February 1913. It did not publish negative reports in the following months, when Mexico and Paribas' syndicate were negotiating the 1913 loan. The prospect of the loan created optimism. *The Times* judged that the operation "will enable the Government to prosecute (the war) with vigour" and to establish "peace within two

[11] *The Statist*, 7 December 1912, p. 673.

[12] *The Times*, 17 January 1913, issue 401107, p. 29.

[13] *PP* Diplomatic and Consular Reports no. 5175, Annual Series, Report for the Year 1912 on the Mexican trade, August 1913, p. 11.

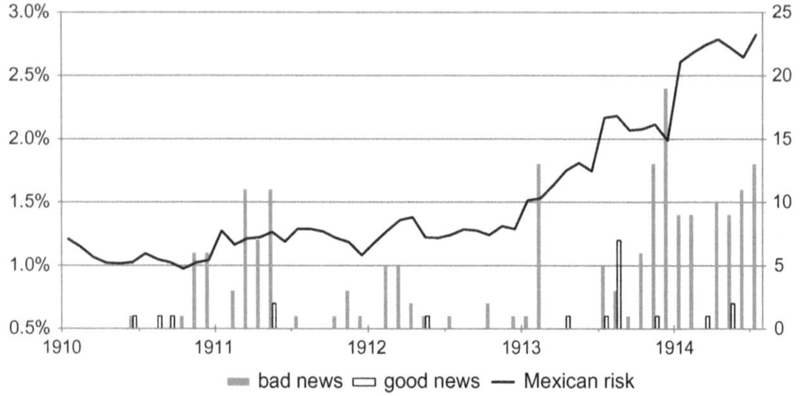

Fig. 8.1 Mexican risk and news from *The Times*, 1911–1914 (*Source* Calculated from *The Investor's Monthly Manual*, *Bulletin de la Côte*, *Mexico* (1925), *The Times*. *Note* Mexican risk on the left-hand side, number of reports on the right-hand side)

months."[14] *The Economist* reported that the loan "gives hope for the speedy restoration of order."[15]

The way bondholders priced Mexico's debt was consistent with the press. Figure 8.1 shows that Mexican risk fluctuated between 1.0% and 1.5% until 1913. That was roughly the same level at which the market traded the debt of creditworthy and politically stable countries, such as Mexico during the heydays of the Porfiriato in the 1900s.[16] Mexican risk started to rise after Madero's assassination, but it remained below 2% until the second half of 1913.

Asymmetry of information between the press and the underwriters only narrowed down after the terms of the 1913 loan went public in June. Mexican risk surpassed 2% in July, when *The Times* described affairs as "alarmist."[17] *The Economist* recognised that the "long civil war (...)

[14] *The Times*, 17 May 1913, issue 40214, p. 29.

[15] *The Economist*, 31 May 1913, issue 40226, p. 1341.

[16] Calculated from *The Investor's Monthly Manual*.

[17] *The Times*, 15 July 1913, issue 40264, p. 7.

has lasted far beyond the expected period and has been carried on with enthusiasm over the northern half of the Republic." It had become clear that "the difference of only 1% between the British Consols and Mexican Bonds" at which these securities were traded earlier that year "was utterly ridiculous."[18] Political conditions deteriorated quickly in the second half of 1913. *The Times* published a record amount of bad news in December, using the word "anarchy" for the first time.[19] Mexican risk finally rose steeply.

Paribas got rid of its Mexican portfolio before the public understood how unstable Mexico was. The bank was in charge of 28.36% of the 1913 loan, the most significant share of the operation. It sold these bonds on the secondary market right after the loan was issued at a 6% margin. The contract established the margin between the issuing discount and the price at which the underwriters were going to sell the bonds on the market, respectively, 90% and 96% of face value. Hence, the bankers expected to profit from the operation. Altogether the bank earned £102,960 from commission and price run-up.[20] Paribas sold other Mexican securities through 1913, realising a loss of £17,213. Hence, the departure from Mexico was overall lucrative. Most importantly, the bank eliminated its exposure before the debt went into default.

It is striking that Paribas decided to abandon Mexico in spite of its business with the country's semi-official bank Banamex. Paribas owned a significant share of Banamex since the 1890s, but it sold those securities before it underwrote the 1913 loan: It held 17.7% of the bank's shares in April 1911, 6.5% in 1912, 1.7% in 1913 and none in 1914.[21] In a letter to the board of Banamex in January 1913, the French bankers justified such decision based on "the political events that trouble the economic life of Mexico (and cause) worries that are difficult to calm down."[22] Paribas liquidated its exposure to Mexico because of the political turmoil.

[18] *Economist*, 5 July 1913, issue 3645, p. 4.

[19] *The Times*, 3 December 1913, issue 40385, p. 7.

[20] *AHP* Relévé Général, 30 June 1913, Billan Général 1913.

[21] *AHB Assemblée Générale* 1911–1914, box 1, folder 5, pp. 53–273.

[22] *AHB* Paribas to Banamex, 14 January 1913, Caja 1, folder 8, p. 299.

The 1913 loan was an escape route that allowed Paribas to profit while departing from Mexico. The lending involved a conflict of interest: Paribas granted the credit the government needed to honour its debt (and sustain its price) while the bank was selling its Mexican portfolio. However, the loan was too limited and expensive to support the government in its struggle to impose a dictatorial rule over the rebels. If anything, the lending made a default more likely in the longer run. Asymmetry of information was key. Paribas profited because the public, exposed to worse information than the bankers, agreed to take a portfolio that Paribas was keen to liquidate.

Speyers and the Nacional Railway

Asymmetry of information and conflict of interest tell why Paribas underwrote the 1913 loan, but it does not explain the rationality behind Speyer' short-term loans. The bonds never appeared on the secondary market, which suggests that Speyer held them at the time Mexico defaulted. The bank issued its first loan in a relatively benign environment in 1912: Fiscal positions were still not in a state of bankruptcy, and the conflict with the insurgents had not yet become an open civil war. The question then is why that bank rolled over the 1912 loan in 1913.

Paribas' syndicate played an indirect role in that operation. While the bankers were negotiating the 1913 loan, Kuhn Loan, Paribas' New York-based partner, asked Speyers to provide Mexico with the "funds required to repay the 1912 bonds." At first Edgar Speyer, the bank's owner, "categorically refused" to do so, but the financiers ended up reaching a compromise.[23] Paribas allowed Mexico to use the long-term loan it was underwriting to repay Speyer' 1912 loan. This appears in the 1913 loan contract, which established that a share of the borrowed funds would "constitute the provisions for the liquidation of several short term obligations of the Government."[24] In return, Speyers rolled over the 1912 loan so that the government had enough funds to honour "the issue of National (sic) Railways Notes."[25] The proceeding of Speyer' loan

[23] *AHP* Kuhn Loeb to Hauser, 17 May 1913, 11/DFOM-221/27.

[24] *AHP* Mexican 1913 loan contract, Article 10 bis, 11/DFOM-221/27.

[25] *AHP* Edgar Speyer to Finaly (Paribas), 26 May 1913, 11/DFOM-221/27. This also appears in *AHP*, Paribas to Bleichroeder, 19 May 1913, 11/DFOM-221/27.

did not leave Wall Street, where most holders of Nacional's debt operated. Before rolling the credit over, Edgar Speyer requested President Huerta "to authorise payment on account of money owed by the Government to the Railway of the necessary funds to enable the Railway to meet its obligations and avoid a default."[26]

The directors of Speyer and Paribas cut this deal as the Nacional railway was about to issue a loan for £5.5 million. Once Edward Speyer agreed to renew the 1912 loan, the Nacional reduced the borrowing to £1.6 million. According to *The Economist*, Paribas's syndicate would have had problems in finding a market for the long-term 1913 bonds had the Nacional issued a £5.5 million loan. The newspaper reported that the railway and the government "compete" for credit and that the Nacional's debt "is possibly a better security."[27] The railway issued its bonds in July, a month after the issuing of Paribas' loan. The agreement among the underwriters cleared the market for the 1913 bonds and prevented a default on the Nacional's debt. Both outcomes helped Paribas to sell its Mexican portfolio at a profit.

Paribas had the upper hand not only over the government but also over Speyer. The contrast between these banks explains this unbalanced relationship. Paribas was a large and well-established European bank (Plessis 1994, 90). Speyer was a smaller but more internationalised American enterprise. It started as a branch of the London-based Speyer Co. and became an independent bank by the turn of the century. According to Carosso and Sylla (1991, 60–61), Edgar Speyer looked for foreign business in an attempt to grow in the New York market, where JP Morgan controlled most US deals. Speyers became international when it underwrote loans for the Nacional railway and the Mexican government in the 1900s. It then funded the Banco Mexicano de Comercio, which intermediated the importation of armaments for the Madero and Huerta governments (Merchant 2006, 241–46). Mexico was Speyer' door to the global market. A Mexican default was, therefore, more of a problem for Speyer than for Paribas. Speyer would not scape as Paribas did; instead, it accepted Paribas' pressure and lent to Mexico in spite of the war.

[26] *AHP* Speyers to Huerta, 23 July 1913, 11/DFOM-221/27.

[27] *The Economist*, issue 40226, 31 May 1913, p. 1341.

Conclusion

The governments of Porfirio Díaz built a reputation that lasted more than the Porfiritato. Madero and Huerta were desperate for cash, but the positive image of Mexico persisted. Paribas profited because its managers understood this change quicker than the public. Instead of narrowing down asymmetry of information, as one would assume from the role of gatekeepers analysed in Chapter 1, the bankers kept it wide to profit at the expenses of the bondholders, who suffered heavy losses.

The government had no option but to accept whatever the bankers offered. Paribas was in a strong position to negotiate the 1913 loan because it had limited exposure to Mexico. It held some reduced amounts of Mexican assets, which it liquidated before the 1914 default. Exposure was also small in terms of reputation: Paribas was a large and diversified universal bank to which the underwriting of sovereign bonds was not crucial. More similar to a twentieth-century bank than to the underwriters that appeared in London in the 1820s, Paribas did not fully depend on the rigid hierarchy of the nineteenth-century sovereign debt market.

References

Archival Sources

AHB Archivo Histórico Banamex, Mexico City.
Contrato de la deuda mexicana en Londres.
Assemblée Générale.
AHP Historique Paribas, Paris.
Projet d'Emprunt Mexicain, 11/DFOM.
Billan Général.
Relévé Général.
PP UK Parliamentary Papers.
Diplomatic and Consular Reports.

Official and Contemporary Sources

Bulletin de la Côte

INEGI. 1990. *Estadísticas históricas de México.* Mexico City: Instituto Nacional de Estadística, Geografía e Informática.

Mexico. 1925. *Coleccion de leyes y disposiciones relacionadas con la deuda exterior de México.* Mexico City: Secretaría de Hacienda y Crédito Público.

______. *Cuentas del Tesoro Federal formada por la Tesorería General de La Federación*. Mexico City: Tipografía de la Oficina Impresora del Timbre.
The Economist.
The Investor's Monthly Manual.
The Statist.
The Times.

Secondary Sources

Beller, Susan P. 2008. *The Aftermath of the Mexican Revolution*. Minneapolis: Twenty-First Century Books.
Carosso, Vincent P., and Richard Sylla. 1991. "U.S. Banks in the International Finance." In *International Banking: 1870–1914*, edited by Rondo E. Cameron and Ivanovich V. Bovykin, 48–71. Oxford: Oxford University Press.
Catão, Luís A. V. 1998. "Mexico and Export-Led Growth: The Porfirian Period Revisited." *Cambridge Journal of Economics* 22 (1):59–78.
Garfias, Luis M. 1997. *La Revolución Mexicana: compendio histórico político militar*. Mexico City: Panorama Editorial.
Gómez-Galvarriato, Aurora F. 2003. "Industrialización, empresas y trabajadores industriales, del Porfiriato a la Revolución: la nueva historiografía." *Historia Mexicana* 52 (3):773–804.
Gómez-Galvarriato, Aurora, and Gabriela Recio. 2007. "The Indispensable Service of Banks: Commercial Transactions, Industry, and Banking in Revolutionary Mexico." *Enterprise & Society* 18 (1):68–105.
Joseph, Gilbert M., and Jürgen Buchenau. 2013. *Mexico's Once and Future Revolution: Social Upheaval and the Challenge of Rule since the Late Nineteenth Century*. Durham: Duke University Press.
Katz, Friedrich. 2003. *The Secret War in Mexico*. Stanford: Stanford University Press.
———. 2004. *De Díaz a Madero*. Mexico City: Ediciones Era.
Knight, Alan. 1986. *The Mexican Revolution: Porfirians, Liberals, and Peasants*. Cambridge: Cambridge University Press.
Leal, Juan F. 1986. "The Mexican State, 1915–1973: A Historical Interpretation." In *Modern Mexico, State, Economy, and Social Conflict*, edited by Nora Hamilton, 21–41. Thousand Oaks: Sage.
Maurer, Noel. 2002. *The Power and the Money: The Mexican Financial System, 1876–1932*. Stanford: Stanford University Press.
Merchant, Anaya L. 2006. "Del Banco Alemán Transatlántico al Banco Mexicano de Comercio e Industria: sindicatos financieros internacionales al final del porfiriato, 1902–1927." In *Mexico y la economia atlantica siglos XVIII–XX/ Mexico and the Atlantic economy XVIII–XX centuries*, edited by Sandra K. Ficker and Horst Pietschmann, 239–268. Mexico City: El Colegio de México.

Plessis, Alain. 1994. "The History of Banks in France." In *Handbook on the History of European Banks*, edited by Manfred Pohl and Sabine Freitag, 185–194. Aldershot: Edward Elgar.

Reyes, Jesús M. 1996. *La Política Económica Durante el Gobierno de Francisco I. Madero.* Mexico City: Instituto Nacional de Estudios Históricos de la Revolución Mexicana.

Sánchez, Fernando Paz. 2006. *La política económica de la Revolución Mexicana, 1911–1924.* Mexico City: UNAM.

Trigger, Bruce G., Richard E. W. Adams, Wilcomb E. Washburn, and Murdo J. MacLeod. 1996. *The Cambridge History of the Native Peoples of the Americas.* Cambridge: Cambridge University Press.

Womack, John J. 1984. "The Mexican Revolution, 1910–1920." In *The Cambridge History of Latin America vol. 5, c. 1870 to 1930*, edited by Leslie Bethell, 79–154. Cambridge: Cambridge University Press.

Weller, Leonardo. 2018. "Loans of the Revolution: How Did Mexico Borrow as the State Collapsed in 1912–1913?" *Economic History Review, forthcoming.*

CHAPTER 9

Conclusion

The governments of Brazil and Mexico were independent players in the sovereign debt market during the first financial globalisation. They were free to decide whether to grant exclusivity to patron banks or to negotiate loans with different underwriters. Brazil granted a monopoly on its debt to Rothschilds, while Mexico issued loans through many different underwriters. Rothschilds was the world's premier bank, so exclusive association improved Brazil's reputation as a borrower and created business connections in Europe. Exclusivity allowed the bank to charge high commissions, but it also increased its exposure, which enabled the government to pressure for rescue loans during the debt crises of the 1890s and 1910s. Mexico only had access to second-rank underwriters. Hence, Porfirio Díaz and his high officials decided to foster competition among European and American bankers to reduce the costs of credit. The nationalist ideology of the Porfiriato also explains that choice. Competition had a price, however: The government received no support in the form of cheap credit during the debt crisis that followed the 1910s Revolution, which resulted in default in 1914.

The study of these two cases provides not only striking contrasts but also some similarities. It shows that both governments took decisions in response to specific payoffs. For decades, it made sense for the Brazilians to maintain Rothschilds' monopoly rather than to negotiate loans with other underwriters. In contrast, the Mexican government negotiated loans with different banks, which was rational given the former's nationalist

L. Weller, *Sovereign Debt Crises and Negotiations in Brazil and Mexico, 1888-1914*, https://doi.org/10.1007/978-3-319-73633-4_9

ideology and the latter's mediocre status. The payoffs derived from each country's payment records, macroeconomic fundamentals, political conditions and state ideology.

On the other side of the debt underwriting market, banks were more inclined to grant exclusivity to governments that had honoured their debt in the past, as association with previous defaulters was detrimental to the underwriters' status. That is the reason why Rothschilds offered its services to Brazil rather than to Mexico: The former was the only Latin American country that had not suspended payments, while the latter had been one of the world's worst borrowers. Reputation was backward looking—it depended on the credit record. Yet expectations on future payment conditions also mattered. Macroeconomic fundamentals and political stability determined the final creditors' demand for bonds. Governments that ran sound policies in peaceful countries issued attractive loans, from which underwriters could profit by selling the debt at high prices on the secondary market. The profits were higher the lower the issuing discounts—the prices at which the governments sold the bonds to banks on the primary market. It is not a surprise that banks were keen to hold a monopoly over the debt of creditworthy governments, so that they could prevent competing banks from raising the issuing price of their debt.

Both cases analysed in this book show that governments had strong incentives to negotiate borrowing conditions to increase the net revenues they received from loans. The Mexican government did not accept a patron bank because it sought to bargain, which it did thanks to its improved reputation in the 1890s and 1900s. Brazil attempted to break Rothschilds' monopoly in the 1880s when the government negotiated a credit line with Barings and Paribas. The combination of a sound fiscal policy and high world liquidity reduced Brazilian risk to its lowest level up to that point. The initiative would have freed Brazil to find better deals away from Rothschilds, but it backfired for the contesting banks lost interest as the monarchy collapsed in 1889. Brazil finally suspended Rothschilds' monopoly in the 1900s. The government took advantage of high coffee prices and the liquidity boom of the *belle époque* to issue four loans in Paris through French banks, which charged lower commission rates than Rothschilds.

The reputation of banks mattered, and premier underwriters were more likely to become the patron banks of good borrowers. Nevertheless, banks still needed to convince governments to give up the benefit of negotiating good deals with other underwriters. Even Rothschilds saw its most exclusive client issuing cheap loans elsewhere. The ultimate goal of the governments of Brazil and Mexico was to borrow cheaply; the association with high-status banks was a means towards that end, not an end in itself. Once a member of Rothschilds' select group, it was rational for Brazilian officials to transform a positive reputation into excellent credit condition, which they did by reaching out to underwriters of lower rank.

This conclusion suggests that Flandreau and Flores' (2009) concept of "brands" may be correct for the 1820s, when information asymmetry empowered debt underwriters, but it is overstated for the turn of the twentieth century. Access more reliable information allowed final creditors to operate independently, which empowered borrowing governments. Depending on their macroeconomic and political fundamentals, governments could issue loans at low commission and high discount rates through the services of second-class banks. What is more, the governments' record mattered more for premier banks than for final bondholders. Mexico's long history of debt mismanagement prevented it from doing business with Rothschilds, yet the public welcomed the loans of Díaz's government in the 1900s, when Mexican risk was not significantly above the risk premium applied to the debt of countries with impeccable records. Bondholders acted in a more forward-looking way than old-style banks, for whom status and seniority were crucial. Such changes allowed Mexico to borrow as cheaply as Brazil in the *belle époque*, even though it did not have access to Rothschilds.

Reputation made governments strong when negotiating loans. The better their status as borrowers, the more they could bargain for good deals. The inverse did not always hold. It was not the case that governments on the edge of defaulting were necessarily frail. Contingent on the relations they had built with banks, debt crises could make governments strong, not weak. Rothschilds underwrote all Brazilian loans between 1850 and 1908. It gained from the monopoly, but its reputation depended on Brazil's commitment to debt contracts. Officials in Rio de Janeiro understood that their patron bank was highly exposed and demanded rescue loans—credit granted below the market rate—during the debt crises of the 1890s and 1910s.

The Brazilian debt crisis of the 1890s was particularly long and severe. Two civil wars, military revolts and intermittent popular riots shook the country. The newly established Republic would have likely collapsed had the government consolidated fiscal accounts, for that would have reduced its financial capacity to fight enemies and co-op local oligarchies.

The government free rode on Rothschilds' credit: High officials pressured for cheap loans so that they could deal with that decade's political turmoil without suspending payments on the sovereign debt. It was not until 1898 that Rothschilds made the granting of credit conditional on the implementation of sound policies. The country had been pacified by then, which changed the government's payoffs. It made sense for officials to prioritise the peacetime goal of maintaining a clean credit record. Rothschilds acted as a power broker, helping policymakers to raise taxes and to appreciate the exchange rate in spite of the opposition of coffee exporters, who were severely hit by the strengthening of the mil-réis. The bank did not enforce conditions on economic policies in the mid-1890s, when politics were unstable, because in that period the government would have most likely defaulted instead of appreciating the exchange rate.

The Brazilian government arranged a second rescue loan in 1914. Falling coffee prices and the outbreak of the First World War made a default imminent. Rothschilds rescued Brazil for the second time, but now the bank did not impose conditions on policymaking. The crisis was the consequence of external shocks, and the bankers expected that the government's finances would soon recover. Yet the government still needed to threat to default to convince Rothschilds to issue a rescue loan. The crisis was longer than predictable because the First World War was not the short conflict contemporaries expected, but the debt did not go into default.

The Mexican government failed to arrange a rescue loan during the civil war that followed the Revolution. It needed a large and cheap lending facility to defeat the insurgents and honour the debt. Paribas, Mexico's chief underwriter at that time, was not significantly exposed to Mexico. A major bank in France, Paribas's overall business did not depend on the debt it underwrote—it remained a major bank even though Mexico suspended payments. Low exposure explains why Paribas did not rescue Mexico. It did underwrite a loan in 1913, but the operation involved limited amounts and expensive terms. This allowed the government to honour its debt for a few months, during which the bank sold its entire Mexican portfolio at a reasonable price, including the 1913 bonds, which Paribas floated on the secondary market at a profit.

Poor payment conditions and turbulent politics made Mexico weak vis-à-vis the bankers, incapable of negotiating a rescuing loan. That outcome could have been different had the government agreed on patron banking in the previous decades. The choice of negotiating loans with many banks was rational ex-anti, for it reduced payment costs in a period when no one anticipated the debt crisis of the 1910s. Nevertheless, it imposed a penalty ex-post: The government could not rely on the credit umbrella of a patron bank to borrow the funds it needed to defeat the Revolution.

Brazil was also in a state of political turmoil in the 1890s, and Rothschilds still provided it with cheap credit. The Mexican Revolution was indeed more disruptive than the conflicts of Brazil's first republican decade, but perhaps the Revolution would not have escalated to a total civil war had the bankers provided the cheap credit that the government needed to defeat the insurgents. It is an open question whether Paribas, Bleichroeder or Speyers would have acted as Rothschilds did in Brazil had one of them been handed a monopoly over the Mexican debt. Their financial capabilities and reputation suggest that they would have probably offered a smaller credit umbrella, although the monopoly would have most likely made these banks larger and more influential. In any case, Mexico would have had a greater chance of receiving a rescue loan in this counterfactual. The fact that Díaz and his officials chose not to have a patron bank mattered.

Governments were strong or weak vis-à-vis banks depending on their reputation and the banks' exposure. The cases of Brazil and Mexico show a number of contrasting combinations. Mexico borrowed cheaply during the Porfiriato because it negotiated loans with many underwriters, but the decision of avoiding a patron bank reduced the government's capacity to borrow cheaply during the Revolution. Thanks to its exclusive association with Rothschilds, the Brazilian government received rescue loans in times of crises. Choices and outcomes differed, but one conclusion holds: High officials devised their approaches to debt negotiation based on country-specific payoffs. Whenever they could, governments took advantage of their relative power over bankers to borrow cheaply.

Appendix: Data and Sources

Cost of Debt

The cost of debt is given by the risk premium, defined as:

$$r_{jt} = YTM_{jt} - \delta_t, \quad (1)$$

where

r_{jt}	risk premium applied to the bond j in period t;
YTM_{jt}	yield to maturity applied to j in t;
δ_t	yield on the British consol (the benchmark) in t.

Maturity varied across bond issues. For this reason, Equation 1 calculates risk premium with the yield to maturity, the return on bonds from a given point t until the final redemption. The data on interests, discount and maturity are from a manuscript compilation of the contracts of the Brazilian loans held at the Biblioteca Histórica do Ministério da Fazenda, and an edited volume by the Mexican government.[1] The return on the British consol is from *The Investor's Monthly Manual*, which is available online thanks to the London Stock Exchange Project of Yale's School of Management.

Following Equation 1, I define country (Brazilian and Mexican) risk, the cost of the credit available for the government on the secondary market, as:

[1]*BHMF* 332/225 and 532, and Mexico (1925).

L. Weller, *Sovereign Debt Crises and Negotiations in Brazil and Mexico, 1888-1914*, https://doi.org/10.1007/978-3-319-73633-4

$$R_t = \sum_j \left(\frac{r_{jt}\kappa_{jt}}{\sum_j \kappa_{jt}} \right), \tag{2}$$

where

R_t country risk in period t;
$\kappa_{j,t}$ market capitalisation of bond j in t; thus $\sum_j \kappa_{j,t}$ is the amount of bonds outstanding in t.

Equation 2 measures country risk as an average of the risk premium applied to all bonds floating on the market at a given time t, weighted according to their respective capitalisation, an information available from *The Investor's Monthly Manual.* Mauro et al. (2006) and Suzuki (1994, 14) also take all floating debt into consideration when they calculate country risk. This methodology captures the heterogeneity among different bonds.

The data on bond prices are from three different sources: *The Investor's Monthly Manual* for all Brazilian debt and the Mexican bonds issued in London, which were the majority, the New York Stock Exchange for the 1904 Mexican loan, and the *Bulletin de la Côte* for the 1910 Mexican loan. The 1904 and 1910 Mexican loans were issued in New York and Paris, respectively, rather than in London.

Fiscal Data

The most complete sources for fiscal data arethe *Balanço da Receita e Despesa da República* for Brazil, and *Cuentas del Tesoro Federal* for Mexico. These official yearbooks discriminate sources of revenue and expenditure, but they are often inconsistent: different volumes report dissimilar figures on total expenditure and tax revenue for the same year. The re-constructed data from Estatísticas Históricas do Brasil (IBGE 1990) and Estadísticas Historicas de México (INEGI 1990) are more consistent and reliable. For this reason, I use both sources in the book. The stock of sovereign debt is from Bouças (1955) for Brazil and Memoria de Hacienda for Mexico.

Note on Currency

The Brazilian currency was the *mil-réis*, or 1$000. Contemporaries denominated large figures in contos, or 1:000$000. Brazil was on the paper standard until the 1900s and the value of the *mil-réis* varied in relation to hard currencies. However, the monarchic government often denominated its accounts in gold *mil-réis*, which was pegged to the British pounds at 27 per pence. I only refer to paper *mil-réis* in this book.

I refer to Mexican pesos as *pesos*. The Mexican peso was pegged to silver until the 1900s, when the country joined the Gold Standard.

References

Archival Sources

BHMF Biblioteca Histórica do Ministério da Fazenda, Rio de Janeiro.
Contractos dos empréstimos em libras esterlinas do Governo Federal, 1883 a 1927, 332/225.
Funding Loan, Acordo do Brasil realizado pelo Governo Dr. Prudente de Moraes em 15 de Junho de 1898, 332/532.

Official and Contemporary Sources

Brasil, *Balanço da receita e despesa da república*. Rio de Janeiro: Imprensa Nacional.
Bouças, Valentim F. 1955. *Finanças do Brasil: dívida externa—1824–1945*. Rio de Janeiro: Ministério da Fazenda.
IBGE. 1990. *Estatísticas históricas do Brasil: séries econômicas, demográficas e sociais de 1550 a 1988*. Rio de Janeiro: Instituto Brasileiro de Geografia e Estatística.
INEGI. 1990. *Estadísticas históricas de México*. Mexico City: Instituto Nacional de Estadística, Geografía e Informática.
Mexico. 1925. *Colección de leyes y disposiciones relacionadas con la deuda exterior de México*. Mexico City: Secretaría de Hacienda y Crédito Público.
———. *Cuentas del Tesoro Federal formada por la Tesorería General de La Federación*. Mexico City: Tipografía de la Oficina Impresora del Timbre.
———. *Memoria de Hacienda y Crédito Público*. Mexico City: Tipografía de la Oficina Impresora del Timbre.

L. Weller, *Sovereign Debt Crises and Negotiations in Brazil and Mexico, 1888-1914*, https://doi.org/10.1007/978-3-319-73633-4

Secondary Sources

Mauro, Paolo, Nathan Sussman, and Yishay Yafeh. 2006. *Emerging Markets and Financial Globalization: Sovereign Bond Spreads in 1870–1913 and Today*. Oxford: Oxford University Press.

Suzuki, Toshio. 1994. *Japanese Government Loan Issues on the London Capital Market, 1870–1913*. London: Athlone Press.

Index

L. Weller, *Sovereign Debt Crises and Negotiations in Brazil and Mexico, 1888-1914*, https://doi.org/10.1007/978-3-319-73633-4

R

The manufacturer's authorised representative in the EU is Springer Nature Customer Service Centre GmbH, Europaplatz 3, 69115 Heidelberg, Germany. If you have any concerns regarding our products, please contact ProductSafety@springernature.com

Printed and bound by CPI Group (UK) Ltd, Croydon, CR0 4YY
30/09/2026
02225653-0002